GIG MINDSET

Hannah –
Hope this Book provides
Some useful insights

GIG MINDSET

RECLAIM YOUR TIME, REINVENT YOUR CAREER, AND RIDE THE NEXT WAVE OF DISRUPTION

PAUL ESTES

LIONCREST
PUBLISHING

GIG MINDSET
Reclaim Your Time, Reinvent Your Career,
and Ride the Next Wave of Disruption

ISBN   978-1-5445-0632-6 *Paperback*
       978-1-5445-0633-3 *Ebook*

CONTENTS

I trust you will treat humanity kindly. At the end of the day, at least for now, it is the individual's skills and abilities that have value. I hope the process that rates and assigns future work is honest and level.

My generation will not yield easily to artificial intelligence algorithms. Our grandchildren may have no choice. You have chosen—or been chosen—to stand on the leading edge of disruption, and I know and trust that honesty and character will guide you.

—JOHN ESTES

FOREWORD

When Dick Fosbury was in high school, he was fascinated with the high jump. The problem was that he wasn't particularly good at it. Neither of the commonly accepted jumping techniques—which involved sailing over the bar face down—allowed him to get any higher than six-feet-three.

When he got to college at Oregon State, which had foam landing pads instead of the sawdust and wood chips common at the time, Fosbury tried something new. As he jumped, he turned over, sailed over the bar upside down, and landed on his back in the foam. He soon cleared six-feet-ten and went on to win an Olympic gold medal with a record-setting jump of seven-feet-four.[1]

High jumpers had been going over the bar face down for

---

[1] "This Day in History," History.com, October 20, 1968, https://www.history.com/ this-day-in-history/fosbury-flops-to-an-olympic-record.

a hundred years until Fosbury decided to flip his orientation and reach new heights. Today, the Fosbury Flop is the only technique high jumpers use.

That's precisely what Paul Estes is doing today; he is flipping the paradigm and finding new ways to tackle problems and improve results. He uses democratized technology and open innovation to find the best people to find novel solutions.

Paul is a pioneer of the Gig Economy. His pursuit of the Gig Mindset not only changed the way he works and lives, it set him on a new path. Now he uses his passion and experience to help companies make these changes as well. His agile, open-system approach is outpacing the work of dinosaur managers who limit their knowledge to people on the payroll.

Paul and I share a passion for this approach. I have also used gig tools to start companies and compete with incumbents. While sometimes this was a financial necessity, hiring freelancers also made my companies more nimble and efficient than our old-school competitors. My ad agency, Victors & Spoils, had twenty-five employees but curated the work of more than 7,000 freelance creatives, allowing us to find prompt and potent answers unencumbered by corporate circumspection. I worked from the outside looking in, so when I met Paul and learned he was using the same approach from the inside looking out, we hit it off right away.

The Gig Economy embraces the idea that we are all entrepreneurs responsible for our own career journey. Paul gets this. He may have spent his career in Big Tech, but he has the mindset of an ambitious small business owner. He values entrepreneurs as problem solvers and independent thinkers who work with urgency and brisk execution, and with this book, he reveals the secrets to taking advantage of that world. Entrepreneurs see the possibilities, not the limitations, and so does Paul.

The benefits are far reaching. Shifting to a Gig Mindset and building broad networks of freelance experts and gig workers brings joy back to our work. Entrepreneurs don't have time for a lot of talk. They like to do. Working with people like that invigorates you, allowing you to rediscover your energy and passion.

It's also a generational issue. Millennials entering the workforce have grown up in this democratized, connected world, and they don't want to work in the same command-and-control environment their parents and grandparents worked in. They are focused on outcomes and getting work done. They aren't interested in sitting in meetings. They aren't interested in working on an assembly line. They want to be on teams that collaborate and solve big problems.

Paul isn't suggesting you take work away from an internal employee who writes one hundred lines of code a day and give it to an external worker to do the same job. Real success is when you engage with an expert freelancer who has figured out how to use AI to write ten million lines of code a day. That's an exponential return. Imagine if that same internal employee now coordinates with ten similar freelancers.

If you're a business owner or a CEO reading this, it's incumbent on you to create the new structures and systems for taking advantage of this. Some of you might see this as an existential threat, but if you find yourself on a treadmill, running faster each day to try and make analog systems work in a digital age, the Gig Economy is a way to get your life and work back. Technology is getting faster, and that's increasing everyone's workload, regardless of the industry you're in. The amount of work some of you are going to be in charge of is so overwhelming that you will have no choice but to turn to freelancers. Those who learn the skills that Paul talks about in this book are going to be the winners in this world of open systems and open tools.

The Gig Mindset will pull back the curtain to reveal the

landscape of this world. It's a future where entrepreneurs don't follow a "career path" but mark their own path through the power of open innovation. I've been in the world for some time now, and I can tell you that the friction has been removed from all our systems and we are free from the analog constraints that many of our industries were built on. We're no longer limited to the knowledge of people we hire. The digital age gives us radical abundance, opportunities, and tools, but we need books like this one from Paul Estes to learn how to best use them.

—JOHN WINSOR

INTRODUCTION

"Your profession is not what brings home your weekly paycheck. Your profession is what you're put here on Earth to do, with such passion and such intensity that it becomes spiritual in calling."

—VINCENT VAN GOGH

On a cold October morning in 2015, my boss asked me to join him for a cup of coffee. A quick one-on-one was nothing out of the ordinary, but he'd never invited me out for coffee before. Something was up.

Honestly, our relationship had been off for a while, and there were serious challenges in the overall business. Our office culture was unhealthy and spiraling into toxic. Without a clear path forward, the team floundered.

This wasn't a place for anyone to do their best work. My boss and I couldn't agree, and our strained relationship put even more pressure on the team. He came from the engineering side; I came from the business side. He thought we were a few features away from unlocking scale, and I wanted to make drastic changes to our business approach.

We'd butted heads since the beginning. He wanted to add more features and call it a day, but I thought we needed to address the core business challenges that were limiting engagement and usage. I pushed the team in one direction while he shouted down to go the other way. I knew it wasn't compatible. He knew it wasn't compatible. Yet we worked day after day to get toward the end goal. Honestly, I saw this cup of coffee as an olive branch. A chance to get back on track, to focus on the company's goals, and to work as a team.

After we ordered our drinks and sat down, he told me plainly, "It's not working out. You've got three months to find a new role."

I don't know how long I sat there in shock. I had just lost my role at a Big Tech company. Sure, there were other opportunities at the company. I wasn't out of the fight, but I'd definitely had the wind knocked out of me.

What made the sting so much worse was that this was supposed to be a great week. My first daughter was due in a few days. This was going to be an amazing time for my family, and my boss knew that. Such is the audacity of the corporate world.

That was it. My career ended before my coffee had a chance to cool off. What the hell had just happened? "You have three months to find a new role." I'd never heard those words before, and they banged around in my head like a bull in a china shop.

I'll be the first to admit I wasn't always a perfect employee. Sure, my track record was solid. I put in the hours and made sure I could stand out as an employee and contributor. I had always delivered what was asked, and I'd been praised for my hard work and the product I delivered. My boss and I had disagreements about methods, but after fifteen years working in tech, I never saw this coming.

It shook me. This wasn't how it was supposed to be. This wasn't the path I had envisioned my entire life.

But why did I think this was the only way?

A COMPANY MAN

I'm a third-generation company man.

My grandfather served as a drill sergeant in the US Army

during World War II. When he came home from overseas, he sold insurance. He worked hard, going into the office every single day, and he built a social contract with his company. When he retired, he had a pension from the insurance company and a few benefits from the Army.

My father worked for the FBI before moving to the private sector. He worked security at Shell Oil, climbing the ranks until he ran the entire division. Again, he put in the years and the hard work, and when he retired, he had a pension waiting.

That was the promise sold to me and everyone in my generation: if you work hard and show up, you can keep the same job your entire life and retire with benefits. The company wasn't just a place you worked; it was a part of your life. You grew with them, rising up the ranks, getting your chance to make an impact.

That was the model I lived by. That was the foundation for my life plan. I wanted the company life.

I worked hard in high school so I could get into a good college. Now, I wasn't an A student, but I did well enough. What I didn't have in grades, I made up for with life experience. I was a competitive swimmer, a radio DJ, and the student body president. Then I went to grad school, making myself more marketable for the type of business

I wanted to land. Then I got a job in my field, with the intent to work hard and earn my way up the ladder.

Learn by doing. It's how I was raised, and it's how I lived my life. That was the surest path to job security that I knew, and it's exactly how I lived my life for the next fifteen years.

Everything I worked on was about experimentation and learning, but I knew I had safety in the golden path my father had outlined.

In the back of my mind, I kept thinking about my daughter. She was days away. All I wanted was to give her the world, to be the provider my father had been for my family.

So that moment, sitting across the table from my soon-to-be former boss, I felt like the foundation of my life was crumbling beneath me. I was going on forty, about to be a father, and my life plan had just been shattered.

I took a few days to gather myself. There, at one of my lowest moments, my wife delivered one of my highest.

My daughter was born a few days later. She was a gift, a wonderful miracle that reset every priority in my head. All at once, I was elated and terrified for the future. I stayed in the room with my wife and newborn, basking in a feeling

I hoped would last. Then reality came creeping back in, along with that familiar anxiety. That night, I took a walk to get some fresh air while my wife and newborn slept.

What was I going to do? Find a new company, pledge my loyalty, and try to climb the ranks again? That path no longer felt so secure. I stood in the cold night air, trying to make sense of the last few days.

I felt overwhelmed by a new sense of personal responsibility. I'd spent so much energy trying to do a good job, hunting for that next promotion, and toiling away every hour I could spare. Suddenly, I had time. I had space. I had agency to reinvent myself and chart my own path forward. The question was what should I do with that opportunity?

In that moment, thinking of my growing family, I started a new journey to find my story. The second my daughter came into this world, everything changed. They were my world, and our life became my sole focus. The skills I had, the job I worked, and the life I provided all surrounded them. I needed to find a path that wasn't just safe but kept me relevant and skilled to continue working and growing.

I had to say goodbye to that old mindset. Goodbye to relying on the company to provide a safe and secure path. It was time to chart my own course, to question the norms and radically change the way I worked.

FORGING A NEW PATH

Over the next three months, I ran through my options. One of the first things I did was engage with a career coach.

Okay, this is a bit of an aside: why don't more people hire career coaches? When you're sick, you go to a doctor. When you're training for a sport, you work with a coach. When you're in legal trouble, you go to a lawyer. There is an entire industry out there to help you orient yourself toward the best career. Why don't more people take advantage?

My career coaches (I had two) were amazingly helpful as I went on this journey. They provided me with the confidence and clarity to charge forward.

I could take the skills I already had and apply them somewhere else. I went on interviews with large companies and startups, and even got a few offers. It was tempting, but there was no guarantee I wouldn't find myself in a similar situation in a few years' time.

I could invest some capital and start my own business. I had friends who worked as entrepreneurs, and they were always excited about their new ventures. I was impressed with the clarity of their goals and the Herculean efforts they managed in order to be successful.

Back in February of 2014, Satya Nadella took over as CEO of Microsoft. He brought a great new energy and voice. The culture felt different, which encouraged me to try and stay. My challenge was to find a new role, and quick.

Not long after, I found myself sitting across from a senior executive interviewing for a chief of staff position. I really wanted the job. It wasn't just security; it was a way for me to keep in the same mindset, to keep the status quo.

I'd had good and bad years at the company, but with good reason. I liked to put myself in places where I could provide value. I took innovative and often ambiguous roles, and the company was constantly changing. That level of flexibility gave me time to shine, but it also led to inconsistent reviews.

I remember telling the senior executive, "If you're looking for someone who wakes up every day and tries to play the ratings and review game, I'm the wrong fit. If you're looking for someone who will work hard, take risks, and bring energy to work, then let's get started."

I got the job, but tech is an inherently unstable industry. Innovations come every news cycle, and even big tech companies had to transform and reorganize constantly to adapt to a highly competitive market and changing customer needs. I'd been in the business long enough that it felt familiar, but I didn't have the certainty about where that left me.

There might not be a perfect job, but I knew what I wanted in life: I wanted a career that challenged and excited me, I wanted to provide value and impact in my company and industry, and—most important of all—I needed to be able to support my family and be a part of our journey.

I also had to find the answers my family would need when they entered the workforce. I wasn't going to convince my daughters to follow the same path as my father and grandfather. They would one day need to understand the evolving, hybrid workforce of the future. They would need to know how to make time to reskill, to stay relevant. In order to teach them to follow this path, I would have to first learn these lessons myself.

WHY YOU FEEL STUCK

If you're reading these words, you've likely been in the same place I was.

You don't feel secure. Technology advances too fast for us to keep up with the constant disruption. You're worried about staying relevant, staying necessary, and making the space to actually have a life, too. You think, *There must be a different way forward.*

You work for eight or nine hours every day, but your productivity stinks. Between pointless meetings, researching new skills, and tedious searching, you barely keep up with the minimum. How can you break out of that mold and actually grow?

You're not alone:

- Only 28 percent of Americans max out their vacation days.[2]

- Twenty-four percent of Americans don't pick up books because they don't have time to read.[3]

- The average American works forty-seven hours a week and reported only six and a half hours of sleep per night.[4]

- Sixty percent of Americans say they do not have enough time to do what they want.[5]

---

2   Megan Leonhardt, "Only 28% of Americans Plan to Max Out their Vacation Days This Year," *CNBC*, April 27, 2019, https://www.cnbc.com/2019/04/26/only-28percent-of-americans-plan-to-max-out-their-vacation-days-this-year.html.

3   Andrew Perrin, "Who Doesn't Read Books in America?" *Pew Research Center*, March 23, 2018, https://www.pewresearch.org/fact-tank/2018/03/23/who-doesnt-read-books-in-america/.

4   Andrew Perrin, "Who Doesn't Read Books in America?" *Pew Research Center*, March 23, 2018, https://www.pewresearch.org/fact-tank/2018/03/23/who-doesnt-read-books-in-america/.

5   Marguerite Ward, "A Brief History of the 8-Hour Workday, Which Changed How Americans Work," *CNBC*, May 3, 2017, https://www.cnbc.com/2017/05/03/how-the-8-hour-workday-changed-how-americans-work.html.

There is a new path—one that leads to more growth, gives you back your time, and shows you a different way to approach your career—and that is by taking on the Gig Mindset. We need to prepare more for the future: we're living longer, working longer, and watching industries rise and fall around us.

I thought I had to choose either my work or my family, but that wasn't the case. I shouldn't have to. I love my work and want to solve big problems, have a solid impact. The constraints of how I *used* to work prevented me from accomplishing goals at the office and at home. I didn't have access to the experts I needed; budgets were locked at the beginning of the year. With the Gig Mindset, I eat dinner at home every night and I make my kids pancakes every morning. (Well, not *every* morning. I do understand the concept of a balanced breakfast.) It's a radical new way of working that just might enable us to have it all.

We need to throw out the old ideas. The company-man or -woman mentality doesn't work like it did for our parents. We must adapt, to evolve into something better.

The ground is literally changing beneath your feet. With new technology arriving seemingly every day, you need to improve your skills and constantly add new tools to your belt. This means more than just software. You need to practice this mentality and train some new mental muscles for the work ahead. Your ability to plan, communicate, and delegate is just as important as your knowledge of the latest programs.

It's easy to feel stuck, overworked, and stressed the hell out. I get it. I was there. It's important for you to know that you're not alone. Whether you're the ground-level employee struggling up the ladder or the executive worried about how to compete and provide value to the customer, we all want to stay relevant so we can stay secure. We want to provide value to the company so we can grow and succeed. We want to build a legacy for our families and our communities.

It's easy to stand on a soapbox and say it, but how the hell do we live it?

In this book, I'll show you exactly that. I'll lead you through this journey, step by step. You'll see how I came to accept this new way of living and working, how it changed my life, and how it has inspired me to take on new projects and future-proof my skills. I'll let you in on the struggles and hardships so you don't have to repeat those same mistakes. We'll hear from other industry leaders how they implemented the Gig Mindset.

Most importantly, I'll make sure you know what to do in order to start growing into this mindset yourself.

THE WISDOM OF EXPERIENCE

As we move through this book, I want to remind you that you are not alone. The changing landscape of the workplace affects us all.

It wasn't that long ago that buying a stranger's clothes on eBay was seen as odd and niche. Nowadays, your grandmother has an Instagram account, you get the office lunch through Postmates, and your commute to work is alongside Uber and Lyft carpools. We're not just buying a stranger's clothes. We're riding in a stranger's car, sleeping at a stranger's house, and hiring strangers for every job imaginable. The Gig Economy brought a structural change.

The Gig Mindset is a way to adapt to those changes. It allows you to grow and evolve, to change *with* the world instead of being changed by it—or, even worse, left behind.

But you don't have to just take my word for it.

I've assembled a group of CEOs and business leaders who will add their invaluable experience and expertise to help guide you on your journey to the Gig Mindset. These industry leaders use the same tools and techniques you're going to learn in their professional lives. With the Gig Mindset, they can do more, get better results, and change the lives of more people.

Allow me to introduce our experts.

Steve Rader currently serves as the deputy manager of NASA's Center of Excellence for Collaborative Innovation (CoECI), which is working to infuse challenge and crowdsourcing innovation approaches at NASA and across the federal government. CoECI focuses on the study and use of curated, crowdsourcing communities that utilize prize and challenge-based methods to deliver innovative solutions for NASA and the US government.

Steve has worked with various projects and organizations to develop and execute over one hundred different challenges. He speaks regularly about NASA's work in crowd-based challenges and the future of work both publicly and internally to the NASA workforce to promote the use of open innovation tools.

Steve has a mechanical engineering degree from Rice University and has worked at NASA's Johnson Space Center for thirty years. Prior to joining CoECI, Steve worked in mission control, flight software development for the Space Shuttle and International Space Station, and command and control systems development for the X-38, and he led the Command, Control, Communications, and Information (C3I) architecture definition for NASA's Constellation Program.

Mike Morris is the CEO of Topcoder, the largest free-lance provider in the world, with more than 1.4 million design, development, and data science experts disrupting enterprise software innovation through competition. He is also global head of crowdsourcing for IT services leader WiPro. Second only to his commitment to family—and perhaps waterskiing—Mike has served in leadership roles at Topcoder since 2002.

An active Boston College alum and engineer at heart, Mike continues to lead the crowdsourcing revolution by empowering organizations with limitless software development possibilities and unprecedented access to Topcoder's talented multinational technologists. A Gig Economy expert, he speaks worldwide about cultivating a passionate community to drive the transformative nature of digital asset development across every industry imaginable.

Dyan Finkhousen leads GE's GeniusLink™ group, a global innovation service provider helping clients improve speed and performance by leveraging expert market methodology.

The GeniusLink Expert Operating System delivers domain on demand. With 21 million experts in their network and over $6 billion in business impact delivered, the group optimizes work with a better division of labor and intelligent automation.

Prior to this role, Dyan served as GE's asset optimization marketing leader—leading the launch of the GE Predix brand, the development of the global advanced manufacturing strategic framework, and coaching business teams on the development of GE Predix™ Industrial internet software and services.

A tenured GE veteran, intrapreneur, and global thought leader for the future of work, Dyan has held senior executive marketing and business management roles in GE businesses, delivering global strategy, business model innovation, and breakthrough performance.

Tucker Max is the co-founder of Scribe Media. He's written four *New York Times* Best Sellers (three hit number one), which have sold over 4.5 million copies worldwide. Scribe Media formed to solve a problem: how to get an idea out of someone's head and into a book without them having to sit down and write. Using his knowledge of the publication machinery, he built a company that pairs authors in need with incredibly talented writers.

He is only the third writer (after Malcolm Gladwell and Michael Lewis) to ever have three books on the *New York Times* Nonfiction Best Seller List at one time. He was nominated to the *Time* magazine 100 Most Influential list in 2009. He currently lives in Austin, Texas, with his wife, Veronica, and three children.

John Winsor is an entrepreneur, thought leader, and global authority on the future of work, the Gig Economy, open innovation, and crowdsourcing. John's ideas, expressed through his writing, speaking, and the companies he's built, have placed him at the intersection of innovation, disruption, and storytelling.

John became the global chief innovation officer of Havas when they purchased his open advertising agency, Victors & Spoils, in 2012. Winsor founded V&S after introducing the advertising world to the practice of cocreation in his role as SVP and executive director of strategy and innovation at Crispin, Porter + Bogusky.

John is currently the executive-in-residence at Harvard Business School's Laboratory for Innovation Science at Harvard (LISH) and founder and CEO of Open Assembly, a company that provides content, community, and strategic advising to organizations, people, and platforms to cocreate the future of work.

Winsor's books include *Beyond the Brand, Spark, Flipped,* and the best-selling *Baked In,* winner of the 2009 800-CEO-READ Business Book Award in marketing.

Winsor is an advisor to the Digital Initiative at Harvard Business School and a regular contributor to the *Harvard Business Review*, *The Guardian*, *Forbes*, and *Digiday*.

THE ROAD AHEAD

Now that you've met the people who will join me in guiding you through the rest of this book, I want to make one point very clear: the Gig Mindset requires work on your part in order to be successful.

In *The Gig Mindset*, you will learn about the Gig Economy and how it is fundamentally changing the world of work. I'll outline the benefits of engaging with freelancers to augment your time and expand your capabilities. You'll read firsthand how my methods changed the way I live my life, from everyday tasks to huge corporate projects, as well as the lives of our panel of experts. Most importantly, I will provide you with a framework to get started, continue forward, and build a process of reinvention.

I've spent the last few years living with this new mindset, experimenting with what it can do for my personal and professional life.

Is it easy? No. Nothing worthwhile ever is.

This book is not a quick fix for a problem. This isn't eight-minute abs. Like diet and exercise, the Gig Mindset takes patience and determination. It takes daily tracking and activity. Most of all, you have to want to change. You have to want that better life.

When I wake up, I think about the challenges in helping people still stuck in the old way of thinking. Why is it so difficult? Then I remember that President Obama had a plaque on his desk that simply said, "Hard things are hard."

The Gig Mindset takes practice. Like mastering any skill, you have to start small and work your way up. If this were a book on weight loss and exercise, I wouldn't suggest starting off with a marathon or CrossFit tournament.

Anything worth doing takes effort. The hardest thing for humans to engage in is change. We're hardwired against it by complacency and comfort. That stubborn attitude helped us survive, but now it holds us back. Don't get discouraged if this takes time and practice. I spent years working at this before I recognized the right and wrong approaches. The amazing thought leaders joining me in later chapters each had their own ways of tackling these problems. Together, we're going to show you what works.

If you're reading this book, you already know that hard work is hard. You're still searching for the space you need to properly balance your work and home life. You've got a growing list of tasks you want to do—or need to do—and you can't find a way to get a hold of it. By the end of this book, I want to show you a new way to live and work.

Right now, however, you probably feel like the ground is swallowing you up. Let's start by figuring out how we ended up in quicksand.

STANDING IN QUICKSAND

"How did you go bankrupt? Two ways. Gradually, then suddenly."

—ERNEST HEMINGWAY, *THE SUN ALSO RISES*

Ken the video editor had a problem. He was years into his career and very talented. Top of his game. He knew his software, knew exactly how much time he needed to put out a quality product, and knew how to shine at work. His problem was quantity—and being a bit of a perfectionist. Even at his best, he could only crank out five or six videos a month.

His problem is one we've all faced at one time or another: scale. At his current level of effort, he could only generate a finite amount of work. Years of trial and error made him efficient, but it still wasn't enough. Ken had created an innovative training video, similar to short social videos I'm sure you've seen shared on one site or another. They were a far more engaging way to train than old methods, so demand shot up. Ken's talent and success forced him to innovate and reinvent.

It's a lot like weight loss. At the start of your journey, the pounds seem to fall away. Then you hit a plateau. The number on the scale remains the same, even though you're still dieting and working out. Ken had plateaued at work, and that made him feel less secure in his job.

It doesn't matter if you're selling, editing, engineering, or managing; you need to keep up with new trends and tools. It'd be great to constantly train in new skills, to up your game so you remain competitive, but who has the time? Between endless meetings, grinding work, and juggling for some space at home, your days are full.

We're all standing in quicksand. The world is literally changing beneath our feet. If we struggle, fighting to maintain control of the old ways, we're going to sink. Right now, with this book in your hand, you have a choice to make. Are you going to wait for the world to make you irrelevant, or are you going to evolve and survive?

DISRUPTION

"If you do not change direction, you may end up where you are heading."

—LAO TZU

The Gig Economy changed the world overnight, disrupting the established model and upending the old way of doing business. *Webster's Dictionary* defines it as a free market system in which companies regularly engage with freelancers or temporary employees for short-term contracts. Where previous generations found a job and stayed with it for decades, many people in today's workforce change jobs regularly, and supplement their incomes with contract-based "side hustles."

Think about the disruption caused by the first iPhone. The week before, your phone had the ability to make and receive calls, do basic calculations, and record a limited number of messages. If you wanted a GPS, that was a separate device. Few phones had the storage for music, let alone other media. Then, almost overnight, you had one device in your pocket that covered all those needs and more.

We take it for granted now, but having the internet in your pocket changes everything. You have access to limitless information and literally millions of applications at your fingertips. That's disruption. Uber changing the way we approach public transportation is disruption. Alexa introducing the world to artificial assistants is disruption. All of these change our expectations and the way we interact with technology.

The Gig Economy is disruptive to the old ways—in a good way. Disruption is a natural process in business. We're living through some pretty radical times, but it can all be for our benefit. One of the biggest changes—and challenges—is the shift to on-demand responsiveness. If I want to watch a movie, I can access tens of thousands at an instant. If I need a ride somewhere, a driver will come to me within five minutes.

It's not just food and products. The Gig Economy opened the door to on-demand experts and services. Sites like Clarity.fm connect people to experts in dozens of fields at the touch of a button. Fiverr provides virtual assistance for a fraction of the price of an in-house employee. Upwork built a network of millions of talented freelancers covering hundreds of skills. While these new companies may drive innovation, older brands are quick to adapt—as we'll talk about in future chapters.

Surviving—and even thriving—means accepting change, and as we've established, change is hard. It's frustrating. I get it. When I felt the ground moving, my first instinct was to resist what my father taught me. To fight back. To dig deeper into my old habits and experiences and sink farther into the quicksand.

If you dig down and work harder, put in eighty hours or more a week, you'll earn yourself a little job security. You'll also set a precedent that is impossible to keep up. Even if you could continue that level of output, would you want to? Where's the space for your family or friends or hobbies? Rather than working yourself to death, you need to innovate and change the way you work. By adapting, rather than just ramping up, you can create the space you need.

Everyone has that one project sitting on their back burner, the one they'd love to get to if only there were enough time. If you create your own space, that project can happen.

THE GIG ECONOMY

In 2019, the term "Gig Economy" made it into *Webster's Dictionary*. Its effects can be felt all around us. An article from Small Business Labs discussed the following:

- Thirty-six percent of US workers participate in the Gig Economy through either their primary or secondary jobs.[6]

---

6   Shane McFeely and Ryan Pendell, "What Workplace Leaders Can Learn from the Real Gig Economy," *Gallup*, August 16, 2018, https://www.gallup.com/workplace/240929/workplace-leaders-learn-real-gig-economy.aspx.

- Twenty-nine percent of all workers in the United States have an alternative work arrangement as their primary job.[7]

- Sixty-three percent of full-time executives would become an independent contractor, given the opportunity.[8]

- Nearly 40 percent of the American workforce now makes at least 40 percent of their income via gig work.

- Over 75 percent of gig workers say they would not leave freelance work behind for a full-time job.[9]

- Fifty-five percent of contingent workers also have a regular or full-time job.[10]

- Thirty-seven percent of full-time freelancers, inde-

7   Shane McFeely and Ryan Pendell, "What Workplace Leaders Can Learn from the Real Gig Economy," *Gallup*, August 16, 2018, https://www.gallup.com/workplace/240929/workplace-leaders-learn-real-gig-economy.aspx.

8   Meghan Heffernan, "Mavenlink Study Finds that Senior Executives, Not Millennials, Driving US Towards Gig Economy," *Mavenlink*, September 28, 2017, https://blog.mavenlink.com/press/white-collar-gig-economy-research.

9   "Understanding the Long Tail of the Gig Economy," *PYMNTS*, May 17, 2018, https://www.pymnts.com/gig-economy/2018/freelance-workers-payments-online-marketplace-hyperwallet/.

10 "Understanding the Long Tail of the Gig Economy," *PYMNTS*, May 17, 2018, https://www.pymnts.com/gig-economy/2018/freelance-workers-payments-online-marketplace-hyperwallet/.

pendent contractors, and consultants are ages twenty-one to thirty-eight.[11]

- Over the next five years, 52 percent of the US adult workforce will either be working or will have worked as an independent contributor.[12]

- At least 90 percent of Americans are open to the idea of freelancing, consulting, or independent contracting work.[13]

- The two most common reasons traditional workers gave for choosing freelance work were "to earn extra money" (68 percent) and to "have flexibility in [their] schedule" (42 percent).[14]

It's a boon for freelancers, who can accomplish almost all of the many new tasks available remotely. It's a boon for organizations as well, since they don't need to worry about office space or equipment for these tasks.

11 MBO Partners, "The State of Independence in America," 2018, https://www.mbopartners. com/wp-content/uploads/2019/02/State_of_Independence_2018.pdf.

12 MBO Partners, "The State of Independence in America," 2018, https://www.mbopartners. com/wp-content/uploads/2019/02/State_of_Independence_2018.pdf.

13 Manpower Group, "#GigResponsibly," 2017, https://www.manpowergroup.co.uk/wp-content/ uploads/2017/10/MG_GiggingResponsibly.pdf.

14 Tiffany Bloodworth Rivers, "10 Gig Economy Statistics You Won't Believe," *iOffice*, February 6, 2019, https://www.iofficecorp.com/blog/10-gig-economy-statistics.

Think of the Hollywood model. Back in the early 1920s, huge studios had writers, actors, directors, and crew—all on staff. The overhead was enormous, but the industry boom made it reasonable. As the years went on, the model changed rapidly. Now, a movie crew is assembled by parts. Producers cobble together a team of talented experts, drawing from a well of unionized employees and putting them on a limited contract. Once everyone signs on, they make a movie. With the film finished and the contract met, everyone goes their separate ways. A major goal has been accomplished and then everyone moves on to their next creative project.

Large companies are waking up to this new model in other industries, too. Well-established, decades-old taxi services saw exponential increases in costs for themselves and their customers. Then an upstart called Uber arrived and used freelancers to mitigate so many of the challenges overwhelming the old model. This meant a more viable profit margin, less expense toward customers, and an instant market stake.

The dynamic changes to the economy have a massive effect on companies unable—or unwilling—to adapt. A study by Innosight found that nine out of ten companies from the 1955 S&P 500 are gone due to changes in the market.[15]

15   Scott D. Anthony, S. Patrick Viguerir, and Andrew Waldeck, "Corporate Longevity: Turbulence Ahead for Large Organizations," *Innosight*, Spring 2016, https://www.innosight.com/wp-content/uploads/2016/08/Corporate-Longevity-2016-Final.pdf.

They anticipate that roughly half of the companies left on the list will be gone in just the next ten years! This demonstrates how the rise of technology, as well as the accelerated pace of change and disruption, has a powerful and far-reaching effect on the economy.

Netflix, already a market disruptor, changed the game again when they introduced streaming. We were all happy with the red envelopes. No late fees? You've got a customer for life. Then Netflix took the mailbox out of the equation. Got a computer? You can watch wherever you are. Same price. That's incredible! Now, just a few years later, Netflix is pushing out original content every month. They control the Hollywood model from pre-production all the way to your living room. Today, they produce more original content than HBO, Showtime, and all the old premium channels.

The Gig Economy has also opened up numerous industries to workers they might never have seen before. Topcoder, for example, utilizes engineers and programmers from around the globe.

These services provide a gateway to a new workforce, one that isn't restricted to an office. Engaging with freelancers is a force multiplier, as you'll learn in an upcoming chapter. Ken the video editor can provide a maximum of twenty-four man-hours a day, but not consistently. He should get some sleep, spend time with his family, and probably eat something.

By working with the Gig Economy, however, Ken can increase his productivity exponentially.

THE FUTURE-PROOF EMPLOYEE

As I told you before, I'm a third-generation company man. However, the world is very different now. I can't follow the same path or learn from the same lessons as my father and grandfather. I am trying to figure it out as technology changes, trying to stay relevant.

We're living longer today, which means we're working later and later in life. Previous generations had to stay relevant until sixty or sixty-five. Now we have to prepare to provide value into our seventies.

When I almost lost my job, it pushed me off the path of the company man and forced me to think differently. I didn't know what I was going to do next, but I knew there had to be a better way. That first step outside of my comfort zone helped me discover the Gig Mindset and think like an entrepreneur.

You see, anyone starting a business must have an idea. A goal. Something they work toward every single day. The mission-oriented mind is often more successful. But just because they have a mission doesn't mean they know how to do every single step to get there. A jack-of-all-trades is a master of none.

Successful entrepreneurs engage with experts for specific tasks, using them to tackle the steps necessary to move toward the end goal. They blend vision and execution and are known for persistence and solving problems. If you were to do the same, what could you accomplish? Hell, what *couldn't* you accomplish?

Four years ago, I faced my own irrelevancy. I had a virtual pink slip. It woke me up, showed me that I needed to take control and bring a new way of thinking to my work. I needed to reinvent the *way* I worked.

First, I saw the growth of technology and how it disrupted the way work was done. I saw millennials and Gen Z joining the workforce with new skills and new expectations. Then I took stock of myself and my skills, and it was sobering. I had fifteen, maybe twenty more years to show up and provide value professionally. To be future-proof, I needed to change the way I approached my work. This was a searching phase, and I exercised my curiosity and started to experiment.

Make no mistake: your relevancy at work is directly

related to your company's relevancy in the market. Every day, technology and business change in a dozen new ways. Cloud-based companies disrupted the old landscape, leading the tech giants to pivot and adapt to the new trends.

Second, I have always worked to provide value to the companies where I worked. There's an old saying: love what you do, and you won't work a day in your life. I was fully invested in my work and my company. I loved what I did and where I did it. My passion remained intact, but I had no outlet for that passion. Like Ken, I had plateaued. I couldn't rely on just showing up and doing work like any other employee. Still worse, I felt like I wasn't providing the impact that I could. At larger companies, it's easy to feel constrained, unable to innovate. I wanted to bring entrepreneurial thinking to the corporate environment the same way Tim Ferris inspired many small business and entrepreneurs to think differently.

It got me thinking: How can I show up every day excited about work, about the way I aid the company and our customers? How can I continue to modernize my skills, have an impact, and create value for the company and our customers?

Third, I had to fight for my daughters. We want the best for our children. We want to build a life for them that is better than our own. Safer. Easier. More than that, I needed to be sure I taught them the right path. That "company-man" mentality might fail me, and I didn't think that mindset would keep me relevant.

I've worked in technology my entire adult life. I've had a new job roughly every two years, and more than thirty-five managers and countless reorganizations as the companies continued to evolve in a highly competitive landscape. All of it made me realize that I had to teach my daughters about the future of business. They were going to face a hybrid workforce of full-timers, entrepreneurs, and freelancers. If I was going to prepare them to succeed, I needed to understand this new economy. I had to make myself the expert.

The futurist Alvin Toffler famously said, "The illiterate of the twenty-first century will not be those who cannot read and write, but those who cannot learn, unlearn, and relearn." In the new economy, you can't pass up the opportunity to learn and grow.

THE HALF-LIFE OF SKILLS

If you went to college, you spent four years learning at least one skill. For Ken, our video editor, that skill made him capable of taking chunks of video and putting them together in engaging ways. It meant learning Avid or Final

Cut or Adobe Premiere, alongside dozens of other software and tools.

The problem is that all of that skill comes with an expiration date.

Stephane Kasriel, the CEO of Upwork, puts the half-life of a learned skill at about five years—meaning that the skill is worth about half as much as it was when you first gained it. In his article in the World Economic Forum,[16] Stephane posited that while many of today's jobs fit a twenty-first-century model, the training and skills were stuck in the twentieth. That rapid pace of change in jobs and skills means there's a growing demand to update skills as well. According to a new report on workforce reskilling,[17] one in four adults reported a mismatch between the skills they have and the skills they need for their current job.

This isn't to say that your ability in them fades, just that the applicability of that skill goes away. Think about bank tellers after the arrival of the ATM, the telegraph operator after the invention of the telephone, the travel agent after

---

16 Stephane Kasriel, "Skill, re-skill and re-skill again. How to keep up with the future of work," WeForum, July 31, 2017, https://www.weforum.org/agenda/2017/07/skill-reskill-prepare-for-future-of-work/.

17 "Accelerating Workforce Reskilling for the Fourth Industrial Revolution," World Economic Forum, July 27, 2017, https://www.weforum.org/whitepapers/accelerating-workforce-reskilling-for-the-fourth-industrial-revolution.

the launch of Travelocity, Orbitz, and Priceline. Time slows for no one, and progress—especially in technology—is constant. If you don't continually reskill, you guarantee your own irrelevance.

The problem, as I'm sure you've felt before, is that there is just no time to reskill. Sure, I would love to learn a foreign language, but when am I supposed to take a lesson? It would be great to be an expert in every task I'm assigned, but I have deadlines to meet and meetings to dodge. (We'll come back to meetings later, but let's just say they should be avoided like the plague whenever possible.)

Freelancers understand this pain point better than most. Because they are constantly looking for their next clients, they tend to ride the trends and fads better than most. After finishing a job, they can use their downtime to reskill for the next set of clients. They learn by doing, and a diverse set of clients means they're constantly working on new ideas and goals.

I understand the benefits of working for a big company. I like the knowable hours and the benefits. But I understand how my old-world job fits into this new Gig Economy. I recognize that I need to make time and reskill so I can stay relevant, and so I can continue to provide value. Recognizing the changing landscape is just the first part of a larger process.

Reskilling isn't just important for white-collar employees. Trade workers have to reskill all the time. Fire alarm technicians have to attend annual updates for software and hardware from companies like Monaco. Meter readers have to learn how to use newer wireless meters so they can function at newer buildings. Plumbers and welders have to obtain safety certifications and train on new equipment. And as the world grows more complex, as the internet connects more and more devices, there are new skills and new ways of thinking required.

You need to make space to learn, so keep these three things in mind: It's up to you to make the *time*, you can learn by *doing*, and you *need* to reskill.

One, everyone is busy. This is just the reality of the world we live in. Information workers have roughly twenty-four minutes a week[18] to focus on training and development. To complicate things further, our modern attention spans are much shorter. People won't read emails that take longer than four minutes. Meetings drain time and energy (and have rapidly diminishing returns). Accept that reskilling is necessary and make time to get it done.

Two, most people learn by doing. The way we live as con-

---

18 Josh Bersin, "Future of Work: The People Imperative," *Deloitte*, October 2017, https://www2. deloitte.com/content/dam/Deloitte/il/Documents/human-capital/HR_and_Business_ Perspectives_on_The%20Future_of_Work.pdf.

sumers impacts how we work. When we try something new, experiment, and collaborate, we tend to learn the skills we need. You have likely picked up new abilities just by interacting with your coworkers and friends over the last year. That human connection gave the skill an inherent meaning and value, which helped you learn faster.

Three, understand that you *need* to reskill. Every company is a technology company now. We live and breathe the internet, communicate on the cloud, and command from a network rather than a central location. This is true all over, so there is no use clinging to visions of the past. You have to learn, to grow, to evolve.

My "aha" moment came with a pink slip, and I was fortunate to jump into a new position and reinvent my professional life. This was the start of a journey and a realization that I needed a new outlook and a new mindset. Learn from me and be open to new ways of working.

THE T.I.D.E. MODEL

It's easy to say, "make space and learn," but it's a lot harder to visualize just how to do it.

That's why I came up with a blueprint for a new way of working that I call the T.I.D.E. Model. T.I.D.E. stands for Taskify, Identify, Delegate, and Evolve. When combined with the Gig Mindset, you can accomplish any goal you choose—and get the results you want.

Once you have your goal in mind, the path is as easy as four steps:

Taskify: Break down your workload into specified tasks.

Identify: Identify what work you must do, drop, delay, or delegate.

Delegate: Find the right experts, communicate your expectations, and delegate effectively.

Evolve: Continue to evolve and grow into the Gig Mindset to make this method work for you and your company.

Remember those four steps, because we are going to spend some time on that path in the chapters to come— and hear from other thought leaders, makers, and doers on how the T.I.D.E. Model helped them innovate and achieve.

THE FREELANCE REVOLUTION

"Teachers will not be replaced by technology, but teachers who do not use technology will be replaced by those who do."

—HARI KRISHNA ARYA, INDIA

A study at Princeton University by Lawrence Katz and Alan Kreuger estimates that nearly 30 percent of jobs in the United States could be taskified—performed by freelancers—in the next twenty years.[19]

You might think that number is a little scary. I want you to try and replace your apprehension with excitement. This disruption may force you to learn and grow, but it will also accelerate innovation.

Remember Ken, our video editor with constraints on his demand? He faced the same concerns. His desire to deliver product of a specific quality meant he could only push out a few videos a month. He had the skills, but he couldn't scale to meet the demand. He needed a solution.

I came to Ken with a proposal. A lot of his backlog came from the early stages of video creation. Writing scripts, gathering assets, creating storyboards, and adding music and sound was tedious work. There were countless websites offering the services of freelance editors to do exactly those tasks, and I introduced the idea to the team. I suggested he do a trial run.

Over the next few weeks, Ken saw the power of scaling with freelancers. He started building a network to tackle

19   Lawrence F. Katz and Alan B. Krueger, "The Rise and Nature of Alternative Work Arrangements in the United States," *Princeton*, March 29, 2016, https://krueger.princeton.edu/sites/default/files/akrueger/files/katz_krueger_cws_-_march_29_20165.pdf.

various parts of the project, creating a system he could scale with the growing demand. Better yet, he learned new skills and made new connections by interacting with talented creatives around the world. When the month was over, Ken had helped coordinate, edit, and polish an incredible number of videos. He increased his output from six to forty-six!

The lightbulb went on. Ken recognized the market value of his videos ($800) and built a system to maximize output. He'd shifted his mentality to a creative director and engaged a small team of freelance experts to work underneath him. The following month, he tasked out dozens of videos. It took time for the trust to build, but soon Ken and his network had their system optimized. He was still working hard, but now as more of a creative director than a video editor. His productivity soared, and the quality of his videos remained at his high standard.

Ken started his journey standing in quicksand. The old way of working wasn't just holding him back, it was dragging him down. By accepting the Gig Economy and engaging in the Gig Mindset, he made himself exponentially more productive and able to provide an even greater impact.

Just imagine what you'll be able to do when you stop hogging the stress of working alone and start sharing the load.

THE GIG MINDSET

"If you want to go quickly, go alone. If you want to go far, go together."

—AFRICAN PROVERB

It was Saturday morning shortly after the birth of my second daughter, and I was working on a slideshow. This presentation had taken months of effort and was bound for an executive briefing. Important work. As I sat there, I couldn't shake the feeling that my priorities were off. I was working on a slideshow while my wife enjoyed time with our daughters.

I was putting my work ahead of my family. Sure, it was an important meeting—a vision presentation to senior leaders across the company—but my daughters were growing up down the hall while I was sinking hours into this presentation. That gnawing feeling grew; that voice in my head got louder. Something was off. I needed a change.

You've probably been there, in that same moment as me. Whether it was a presentation or a major project, you prioritized your work over yourself and your family. That's messed up, right? It's upside down. Even if you love your work and love your company, you're wasting a perfectly good Saturday and losing valuable time with the most important people in your life.

At that moment, I suddenly remembered advice from a friend of mine, Adam Benzion. He was a serial entrepreneur, which meant that every second of his day needed to be planned out working with his startups. He knew time management because it would make or break his business. I remembered that he had told me to get a virtual assistant. At the time, I probably logged it away as a cool idea, not really something I needed. That Saturday morning, his advice sounded like a starting pistol.

I took a break from my presentation and went online to a website called Fancy Hands. Finding a virtual assistant was quick, and suddenly I had a second set of hands to chase down whatever I needed. That begged the question: what did I need?

I knew exactly what: family time.

I felt guilty about letting my work life encroach so much at home, so I asked my new assistant to find an activity for my family. I told them I wanted somewhere close, within five miles of my home, where I could take my wife and daughters. Immediately, my assistant went to work. While I had time to finish my presentation, this other person searched all the local events and put together a short list for me. An hour after I made my request, I got a message back. There was a strawberry festival only ten blocks from my house.

Could I have found that on my own? Of course. The festival wasn't hiding. I can type words into a search engine as well as the next person, but it would have meant an hour fumbling through different sites, getting lost down rabbit holes, ending up with search fatigue. With my virtual assistant, that hour still belonged to me. They were able to curate something based on my specific needs.

I spent my Saturday finishing that report. The next day, I took my family to the strawberry festival. It was a magical day, filled with music and face painting and games. It was a day when my priorities were on target. More than that, it opened my eyes to the possibilities of the Gig Economy.

My wife and I spent many years in corporate America. I'm constantly writing articles or working on book concepts. We are a very busy family. Yet for one day, with just a little help from a virtual assistant, I was able to make the space I needed to take care of the people that mattered most. Lightning struck my brain. What else could I do? If I was able to affect my personal life in such a positive way, imagine the effect it would have on my work life.

We're living in a freelance revolution. There are so many services that you've likely only scratched the surface. Maybe you Uber instead of taking a cab. You order your food through Postmates or Grubhub, your groceries from Instacart, your clothing from Stich Fix. You get graphic design from 99designs or a website built through Upwork. For every site you know and use, there are hundreds more waiting to be discovered. With the Gig Mindset, those resources open your world in a brilliant way.

I don't search the internet anymore. Every morning, I jump on Fancy Hands and set up a few tasks. By lunch, I have the responses I need. By dinner, those tasks are complete. I use ten minutes of my own time and get a day's worth of effort.

It's like the first time you got a red envelope in the mail and knew that video renting would never be the same. Or when you saw the iPhone and realized a world of information could be in your pocket. The Gig Mindset changes the way we work forever. It allows us to use on-demand experts to reclaim our time. When I realized that, when I saw how technology multiplied my capabilities, I knew that the future—my future—would be different.

My first day with the Gig Mindset, I used a single expert to locate a strawberry festival a few blocks from my house. Now I use a network of experts, and it has opened up my schedule for the things I care about: I have time to exercise; I can help my daughters with their homework; and I can spend quality time with my family.

My time using freelancers led to a new way of thinking for the workplace. Just as the Gig Economy changed expectations about on-demand services, so too the Gig Mindset changed my expectations for business. This wasn't exactly a radical development. We've seen it happen with the consumerization of IT.

Information technology is a critical function of any modern workplace. If you don't believe that, check the mood of any office before and after a printer unexpectedly crashes or when the network is too slow. Consumerization is more than just personal consumer electronics at work—like iPhones and tablets—but is also in online services: online data storage, web-based email, social media, and social networking.

This change started with employees bringing their own devices to work, connecting to the corporate network, and demonstrating the change in efficiency. That led to companies adopting those practices as standard operating procedure (SOP). In the same way, imagine the

Gig Mindset being brought into the workplace. Imagine employees arriving with their own networks of freelancers, prepared to adapt to any challenge.

If the Gig Mindset works this well for me as an individual, imagine what would happen if every person on your team lived it as well. What happens when every employee brings their own network of freelancers to the job?

I'll show you.

THE INTERNET BREAKS THE MOLD

In just a few years, Netflix went from 12 million subscribers in 2011 to 139 million subscribers worldwide in 2019. When they launched a global network, that number jumped again. Now they are known not only for the content they share, but also for the original series and films they create.

The internet changed everything. I know, that's not exactly news, but it was a while before I realized just how much the internet altered our way of interacting with the world. Do you remember your first time in an AOL chat room? Or using early search engines to gain instant knowledge?

You might not remember, but Netflix used to have users

play a little game when they first signed up. They presented you with a series of films, and you would rate the selection if you had seen them. Netflix called the service Cinematch, and it was a simple algorithm that recommended movies based on your history. It was...mostly accurate. With 35,000 titles to choose from, they can't all be winners.

In 2006, Netflix wanted to update their algorithm. Rather than hiring a software company for millions of dollars, they went to the internet. Netflix put out a call for a competition to beat their algorithm, and they put up a $1 million prize for the winner. They embraced the growing Gig Economy and saved money at the same time.

It's not just new industries taking advantage of the changing times. Taxi companies face increasing costs at every end. Roads are more congested, vehicle maintenance and insurance is more expensive, and the value of a licensed medallion has skyrocketed. This has caused fares to increase dramatically, dissuading customers and killing the bottom line.

Enter Uber, a ridesharing service that disrupted the taxi industry immediately.

If you want a cab, you have to call a company. You have to know exactly where you are. You have to know the exact address of where you are going. Many cabs prefer cash over credit, and there's always an argument over how much to tip. With Uber, you only need a smartphone.

It's been just ten years since most of these companies started, and they have already had a huge impact on our lives. You step out of a building and press a button on your phone. The GPS on the phone identifies where you are and automatically places a pin down. You type in an address and the phone automatically completes the necessary information. You're shown a picture of the car, the driver, and the license plate at the moment the ride is accepted. Once the trip is over, you press another button to pay the driver. That's it. No stress, no math, just a simple ride from a friendly stranger.

This led to the "Uberization of Everything." From hotels to travel to employment, new companies arose to provide on-demand access to the services we use every day.

The internet is a marketplace where old problems are workshopped, solutions are proposed, and businesses rise to fill the void. If there is something you need done, there is someone out there ready to help. All you need to do is understand how to find them.

EMBRACING THE GIG ECONOMY

Did you know that there is an app for your phone that will, with the press of a button, order someone to come and walk your dog?

Isn't that amazing?

Dog walkers are nothing new. They exist because dog lovers have jobs and cannot be home to care for them 24/7. These animal-friendly freelancers come to your home, collect your pets, and take them for a little exercise.

You might be wondering, "Paul, why do I need a company for this? I could go online and search for a dog walker and order one myself. I'll bet there are yellow pages for that sort of thing."

Okay, so you want to do a little legwork? Admirable. But how are you going to vet these dog walkers? Do you know their safety records? What about personal testimonials from customers? How many emails will you need to send? How will you handle payment? Sure, you could do all of that yourself, but how much time did you spend tracking it all down?

The Gig Economy pushes companies to innovate around those very same problems. Uber and Lyft run background checks, use customer data to sort drivers, and push all that information to your fingertips. The same is true of these dog-walking services. Each walker comes with a profile, customer reviews, and a list of certifications. All at the touch of a button.

The benefit of using a freelancer is obvious. Having a temporary expert in a specific field provides flexibility, while bringing in knowledge and skills you might not have internally. These networks also enable you to scale rapidly. That's the Gig Economy, and it's only the beginning.

Let's say you're getting hungry after sitting here reading this amazing book for hours. What would you like to eat? In the old days, you'd have a drawer filled with menus from local restaurants. If you're not feeling too lazy, maybe you drive to a fast-food place. All of this ends with something greasy on your plate, which is probably not the best meal you could have.

Today, you can order fresh groceries delivered directly to your door. Whole Foods and a number of grocery stores offer personal shoppers. For a minimal fee, they will pick out your order, pack it up, and drive it right to you within a few hours. You can even give personal preferences such as your favorite recipes or the ripeness of your avocados. There are also subscription services like Blue Apron and HelloFresh that curate meals and send them—along with careful instructions—right to you.

Maybe you don't feel like cooking tonight, but your favorite eatery doesn't deliver. In the old way—well, you just wouldn't get to eat your favorite food tonight. Tough luck. Today, we have companies like Grubhub and Postmates ready to collect and deliver just about anything you can ask for. If you want McDonald's with Krispy Kreme for dessert, they can make it happen at the touch of a button.

Our expectations are changing rapidly. Amazon now provides same-day delivery in some locations. None of this innovation came easy. These companies did the hard work, and now they've enabled their customers to enjoy on-demand service.

All of this sounds fun, but it also means time saved. Instead of waiting in traffic, stopping at a restaurant, placing an order, waiting for it to be cooked, and driving home, you get to be at home. You're spending time with family. You're researching for a big report. You're working on that novel.

Instead of running through all of those tasks, you have space to focus on what's important to you. Imagine what you could do with an extra half-hour of space every day. Think about those hours piling up. Whole days of freedom for you to tackle the projects that piled up for so long. What is it you want to do?

I DON'T KNOW HOW

I just saw a great commercial for tax preparation. It was by Intuit, the company that owns TurboTax. Every year, they put out commercials touting how simple they are to use. This year's update means doing your taxes only takes five minutes! Now with free grammar checks! Every deduction comes with a free mint delivered right to your door!

TurboTax isn't the only product on the market, and the escalation of coupons and free services can only go so far. So how did Intuit stand out? How did they deliver a better experience to people who want to spend as little time doing taxes as possible?

They advertised that they were putting CPAs in the software—that would be there on demand to help you while preparing your taxes—touting "You get a CPA, you get a CPA."

Taxes aren't fun, no matter what your uncle the CPA tries to tell you. It's a lot of math, the rules change every year, and if you get them wrong it's a real pain. It's a stressful point for many people, and having a real human being able to walk you through can be a game changer. That's why H&R Block is still in business. They offer the comfort of an expert, albeit for a bit more than a free online service.

By adding the ability to connect on demand with an actual expert at the exact time you needed assistance, Intuit changed the nature of their product. They weren't just offering an inexpensive way to do your taxes. They were telling you that they had your back. If you had a question about this important process, an expert would guide you through.

This is the essence of the Gig Mindset. Take any task, break it down into steps, and find the experts you need to handle each part. In this instance, you need to do your taxes.

Another great example is IKEA. That company already changed the furniture industry by selling their products completely disassembled, passing the savings to the customer. However, the running joke is how difficult it can be to put it all together. Some of their more complex items require at least two people for safe construction—or more than two, if your wife spends most of the adventure rolling on the floor laughing while you fail to construct a crib.

Enter TaskRabbit, a company that offers handyman services. In 2017, IKEA acquired TaskRabbit to offer in-home assembly on demand. At the time of purchase, you can package a deal so a team shows up, builds your furniture, and leaves you in peace.

This sort of product is known as "Last Mile" service, and you've probably taken advantage of it before. Best Buy purchased the Geek Squad for at-home installations and troubleshooting. Home Depot offers their Pro Service. Shutterfly has designers to help you complete your photo books. Google and Amazon integrated a variety of home services for their virtual assistants, allowing customers to access dozens of services with just their voice.

This is wild! Even a few years ago, this level of integration was a dream. A fleeting hope. Now, through the Gig Economy, large companies can engage with specialists and experts to provide even more service to their customers. Upwork, Fiverr, Uber, Lyft, WeWork, Slack, Zoom, and Airbnb all are built around the idea of connecting people. What makes this moment even more important is that now, in the past year, these companies have gone or are planning to go public. They're entering the market to accelerate an already changing environment.

That is the essence of the Gig Economy: connecting people and trends together. All of these new companies—from Upwork and Fiverr to Lyft and Uber—revolve around the idea of connecting people together.

It's not just about providing service to customers. It's a restructuring of how we connect to get things done. This will impact our personal lives as well as change the way we work. The sooner you recognize that, the sooner you can change your mindset for the future.

It's the Year of the Gig Economy.

YOU'RE GONNA NEED A BIGGER BOAT

When the Gig Economy took over, a lot of large companies only saw it from B to C: business to consumer. That's when Uber and Lyft were first blowing up. Older companies saw this and said, "Well that has nothing to do with us. We can't 'Uber' our industry." After adopting the Gig Mindset, it was clear that the way I worked was broken. I started exploring B2B companies—entities that focus on business-to-business services—and saw the opportunities waiting; that I could change the way I worked and lived. I wanted to share this idea, to inspire others. That's why I wrote this book.

Make no mistake: the Gig Economy is as big a change as the arrival of the internet.

People have trouble connecting to it. That's understandable. Large-scale change often moves in ways we can't easily see. It's the difference between watching clouds drift overhead and watching a massive storm front roll in. With something that massive, you hardly notice the change until suddenly it is all around you.

Look back at the quote by Ernest Hemmingway in chapter 1: "How did you go bankrupt?" Two ways. Gradually, then suddenly." (We'll come back to that quote a lot, so you might as well highlight it now.)

The Gig Economy may have first found scale in the ride-sharing and food delivery space, but its scope reaches far wider.

When you factor in companies like Upwork, Toptal, Fiverr, Airbnb, Business Talent Group, Topcoder, and dozens more, the big picture gets clearer. It's not just the quantity of talent, either. As Ken discovered when creating his training videos, these are professionals at the top of their game. Suddenly, you're looking at a mobile, gig-based workforce of talented experts able to multiply the abilities of your staff.

More than that, this is about the trends created and molded by the Gig Economy. Bill Gates famously said, "We're going to put a PC on every desk," back in the 1980s. Then came the internet, connecting people in their homes. Smartphones connected people instantly around the world, and social networks created the platforms to build communities. These innovations fueled the new economic model.

It takes time to turn a big ship, and the global economy

is one hell of a big ship. These freelance companies were started with VC funding, and that's where some remain for years. Now that many are going public, we're about to see another evolution to the model: collaboration within larger industries.

As with Intuit or IKEA or Whole Foods, large companies are embracing these on-demand services to provide new and unique services to their customers. Employee benefits now include access to expert advisors, discounts on numerous applications, or training through a variety of reskilling sites.

This is a big change. It's important that you understand just how much growth is possible. In the few short years since this evolution, we've already seen major companies jump on board the Gig Economy. The question, and the reason you're holding this book, is how can you make this work for you?

If I wanted to sell you on a product, this would be the moment where my fun anecdotes turned into a pitch. I've been where you are now. I know that frustration, that idea that I've been going about my life and my work the wrong way. I want you to know that you're not alone. Your efforts haven't been wasted. And, just like you always suspected, there is a better way.

That's what went through my head during that strawberry festival. I was my own door-to-door salesman, only I was banging on my skull trying to be let in. All my life, I'd lived one way. Planned one way. Thought one way. And suddenly, on a fantastic outing with my family, it all clicked. I had been so wrong.

Now I have a network of talented professionals, and I get to learn new skills every day. It's a wonderful feeling, especially since I am working on keeping my skills relevant while still making an impact. I do believe that companies need to change, and they can. It all starts with understanding that the *way* we work is broken.

The only thing I had to give up was that old mindset.

A NEW STATE OF MIND

"No matter how brilliant your mind or strategy, if you're playing a solo game, you'll always lose out to a team."

—REID HOFFMAN

In December of 2018, my daughter had a high fever. If you're a parent, you know that nothing matters when your kid is ill. The world stops moving, and you focus 100 percent on that child. There are no obstacles. Except that sometimes the doctor's office is closed, or they can't see you until the next Tuesday, or a referral is required. In my case, the obstacles also included piles of snow outside my door.

Well, I'm a dad. And my kid is sick. Snow doesn't matter. How am I going to get around it?

At the time, my company's medical plan had been updated. Along with all the usual bells and whistles, employees had access to an app called Teledoc. It connects patients with doctors for nonemergencies via their smartphones.

Now, as I said, I'm a dad with a sick kid. But I'm also an early adopter, so I had the new Teledoc app on my phone. There was no risk. If I didn't like what the app had to say, I still had the option to try and drive to the hospital.

We clicked the button, opened the app, and suddenly there was a doctor on my phone. Not a computer, not a series of questions, but a human doctor with years of experience. He performed the consult right there, through the app. We spoke for a few minutes, talked about my daughter's symptoms, and he asked some questions to home in on a diagnosis. Once he was satisfied, he called in a prescription right then and there. I was able to get the medicine that day, after the snowplows had done their work.

That's when everything came together.

You see, when I needed something for my family, I had an expert at my fingertips. When I needed to plan a day trip to the strawberry festival, a virtual assistant had my back. When I needed help planning a slideshow or researching a difficult topic, skilled freelancers were a few keystrokes away.

All of this happened because of the Gig Economy. It has different names like telemedicine, ridesharing, and food delivery, but at its core it is matching people to services via platforms. That made me realize that *anything* was possible. I had just discovered a superpower.

I started looking at my life as a series of tasks. Every day, there were tasks I needed to do: repairs to the house, plans to make, errands to run. Every day, I had projects at work: research to do, countless reviews, and never-ending meetings. Every day, I had goals I wanted to achieve but only a finite amount of time to do anything.

So why was I wasting my time on tasks I didn't know how to do—or didn't want to do, or didn't have *time* to do—when there were people who were willing to help?

In any given day, I may work with the following sites (these are just a few):

Upwork: World's largest freelancing platform where

businesses and independent professionals connect and collaborate remotely.

Fancy Hands: US-based virtual assistants that work on tasks and can make phone calls to set up appointments and reservations.

Fiverr: Marketplace of freelancers. They have scoped projects for web development, transcription, writing, and web research, and I've even had caricatures done of my family.

Clarity.fm: They provide expert advice from hundreds of disciplines. At a moment's notice, you can speak with a live human about any issue. This is your personal phone-a-friend.

Ask Wonder: How many times have you wasted hours researching topics on your own? Ask Wonder is a pool of professional researchers able to provide information on any topic in a reasonable amount of time.

This can all seem like a lot to take in. Changing your mindset isn't easy, but it's very possible. I'm proof that the old dog can be taught new tricks. You may stumble, as I most certainly did, but with practice you'll find your way.

The Gig Economy spawned hundreds and hundreds of

small companies that collected together a limitless well of experts. It's time to tap into that resource, reclaim your time, and rethink what's possible.

First? You have to forget everything you thought you knew.

GO-DOS:

1. Make a to-do list. Take out a piece of notebook paper and start thinking about tasks you have put off, where you could use a little help, a passion project, or an organization where you volunteer.

2. On a new page, draw a line dividing the sheet in half. Using your to-do list, separate items from your personal life and for your professional/side hustle.

3. Hop online and explore some of the services mentioned in this chapter. As you get familiar with them, make a note on your list of which services could apply to each to do item.

4. Now try one task on one platform.

RESETTING YOUR DEFAULT

"Opportunity is missed by most people because it is dressed in overalls and looks like hard work."

—THOMAS EDISON

I want to tell you about the Busy Trap.

It's easy to get caught up in everything around you, chipping away at your time until there is none left. You wake up, you go to work, you go to bed, and suddenly a few weeks have passed, and you haven't made any progress for yourself. Your family is getting left behind. Your personal projects are abandoned. That's the Busy Trap, and it catches us all at some point or another. That leads to stress, anxiety, and mental health concerns that cause every aspect of your life to suffer. Not to mention the strain on your personal relationships.

As I started exploring the Gig Mindset, I realized just how much of my life required a redesign. I needed to look at every aspect of my day differently. Speaking with people around the country, I found that my own experience wasn't so rare. I visited Fortune 500 companies, spoke at conferences, and heard from many employees. They wanted innovation and reinvention.

We all had this same connection: we're all stuck in the Busy Trap. We had no extra time for our families or ourselves, no time to reskill or grow. No matter what we were searching for—whether in our individual or professional lives—we knew there had to be a better way.

After a speech at a conference, I remember a woman approached me with tears in her eyes. Literally, tears in her eyes.

"Do you have a minute?"

I immediately saw that she had a need, something weighing her down. I said, "Yeah, how can I help?"

As we chatted, she told me her life story. She was a single mom, working a high-stress job. More than that, she was passionate about her work. It's what she wanted to do. There was just no time for her to destress, to reorganize her life into something more manageable.

She felt stuck. On the one hand, this was her dream job. Working at this company was the culmination of years of hard work and study. She enjoyed what she did and the people around her. The problem was that she couldn't find the balance to get it all done. The demands of her family and her work overwhelmed her. That kind of stress resonated with me. I recognized it since I'd experienced the same challenges.

At one point I asked, "How can I help?"

She didn't know. She knew that things weren't working, but she was too close to the problem. She couldn't see the forest through the trees. Everyone gets here at some point. Your to-do list grows so large that it becomes insurmountable. Just a mountain of tasks you'll never accomplish. At least not alone.

"What is one task on your list that we can get done today? Let's pick a project, just one."

She thought for a moment. I could feel her stress as she ran through a mental list of errands and chores. Finally, she looked up. "I've been really trying to book this trip to visit my parents, but I just haven't gotten to it."

Easy, right? Couldn't she just go to Kayak or Travelocity, type in the cities, and get what she needed? This is the problem with the Busy Trap. A task like this might take only a half-hour or so, but where is that time coming from? Remember, most people only have twenty-four minutes a week to focus on training and development. A single mother working in tech might have twenty-four minutes a month, and certainly not all at once.

Being a parent is a full-time job. You can't request a sick day, you can't take a quick fifteen, you can't leave them while you go off to lunch to decompress. It's a twenty-four-hour-a-day gig. Having a partner provides you with a little space, a chance to catch your breath. If you're a single parent, it's all on you.

This isn't to say that you can *only* experience the Busy Trap as a parent. Some of you reading this book know the feeling just as well because you work long hours, or have numerous side hustles, or can't seem to make time for family and friends. This sadly isn't a unique experience, and we've all thought that there must be a better way.

I grabbed my computer and logged onto my virtual assistant service and typed in the request. It took about an hour for all the information to come together. Once my assistant gathered the details on the best-priced flights, a rental car, and a few options for an Airbnb close to her parents' apartment, I sent them to the woman's email. It took maybe a couple minutes of actual work on my part.

Her eyes went wide. I knew that look. I'd worn that look years before. I've seen it on countless people since I started speaking about the Gig Mindset.

When you're in the Busy Trap, it's easy to feel alone. You think of your to-do list as something that only you can manage, that no one else would ever be able to help with. Once you open your eyes to this new mindset, the truth is easy to see. There are people out there, at your fingertips, ready to assist. Any task, any project, any need can be solved by engaging with talented freelancers.

That woman didn't just see me use a website and solve a problem; she saw the space it created. She saw the time I had given back. She saw exactly what the Gig Mindset could do.

With time and space, anything is possible. Imagine what you could do with a few extra hours. In my experience, using these methods earned me an extra ten days a year to focus on goals that I wanted. That's 192 hours I didn't have before, used the way I wanted to use them.

But it's easy for me to preach to you about what you should and shouldn't do. It's like a fitness guru shouting to stop eating those greasy burgers and donuts. The talk is easy, but the practice is a little trickier. The question is, can you reset your defaults?

IT'S NOT EASY, BUT IT'S WORTH IT

Have you ever quit a diet?

Of course you have. Everyone has. It's a universal experience. Maybe you were trying to lose weight or just wanted to cut out certain foods, but you set up a list of dos and don'ts and tried to stick to it. And failed.

Well, not failed. I don't want you to be too hard on yourself. In any case, that diet did not last.

Most quick fixes fail because they are inherently unsustainable. It's the difference between me asking you to walk a little faster or run as hard as you can. If you sprint full out, how far will you actually get? I'll bet not very. Maybe a mile? Now try walking just a little faster and see how much further you get. It might take longer, but it's sustainable. You could do that all day.

That's the difference between a diet and a lifestyle. If you read any books on Paleo or Keto, they'll all say the same thing: you can't do this just for a little while or just to reach a specific goal. You have to live this way. This has to be your new normal. Otherwise, in your head, you've already quit. You've given yourself permission to fail.

Mindset adjustment is no different. You need to make a point to live the Gig Mindset all the time, not just when it strikes you. Plan to operate around it, engaging with freelancers every single day. Make this your new normal, and it will be.

Just like with lifestyle changes, altering your mindset is easier when you've got a support network. Whether it's your family, your friends, or your coworkers, sharing the journey makes it enjoyable. When you stumble, you have a safety net. When you have questions, one of your peers will likely have the answer.

When I introduced the concept to my team, I found that many of them already had the same concerns and challenges. We were all stuck in the Busy Trap. As we grew and learned together, we built up energy to keep it going. We celebrated our successes as a team, and that made it easier to keep going.

In 1960, Dr. Maxwell Maltz stated that it takes about twenty-one days to make or break a new habit. In 2009, a longer study found it's closer to sixty-six days—on average—for you to reset your defaults. Granted, it varies from person to person, so don't feel discouraged if it takes you longer. But think about that.

Sixty-six days. Just over two months. You could do that. Just eight weeks of logging onto Fiverr or Upwork, eight weeks of sharing the workload, eight weeks of engaging with freelance experts. You'll wake up in the morning and order your groceries on Instacart. Before going to work, you pick out some new clothes through Stitch Fix. When you get to the office, you'll call up Clarity.fm for some research and Fancy Hands to juggle other tasks. Suddenly it's not a chore. It's easy. You're doing this in your sleep. One day you'll wake up, and the Gig Mindset will be your only mindset. You'll have reset.

Like a diet, it's easy to fall back into old habits. Sure, taking care of individual needs with the Gig Mindset comes naturally. We're already used to other people making us food, driving us around, or answering questions online. That's basic. What happens when you encounter a bigger problem? What happens when you get stuck with a major project at work and you need to spend time after dinner instead of planning the weekend with the family?

This is where a support system comes into play. First of all, you have this book. I'm here as your guide to walk you through the first couple of projects and set you on the right path. If you run into trouble, I can all but guarantee I've already been there. In fact, if you look at the back of this book, you'll find a list of projects I've already tried and completed that you can follow.

Second, you'll have the stories of the thought leaders I've assembled. From GE to NASA to Topcoder, I've brought in some brilliant innovators to share their war stories and inspire. If you're struggling to see the forest through the trees, they're here.

Finally, you have a community in the making. Wherever I go to speak, I'm met with people who are stuck in the Busy Trap. They've all got the same to-do list looming over their heads, and they all cheer when I show them how to get out from under it.

You are not alone in this. Not ever. We're here to get shit done. The way we do that is by reclaiming our time. And the best way to reclaim your time is to stop wasting it. Take ownership of the hours you have in the day.

DEATH TO MEETINGS

Can we all agree that meetings are just awful? You sit in a windowless conference room with a bunch of coworkers, you listen to presentation after presentation, the leader wanders from topic to topic with no regard for the agenda, and then you leave a few hours later with nothing gained. They suck. They're often completely pointless, and it would have been better to send an email with the information. That's why I decided I'm not going to them anymore.

Okay, let me qualify that. I'll do work that requires collaboration, because not every problem can be solved via email. If they follow the well-established rules for productive meetings, I'm fine. But otherwise, I'm cutting myself out of as many meetings as possible. I'm reclaiming my time in the easiest way: by not wasting it in endless meetings. It is not always easy to decline meetings, but I am open and honest about where I can provide value and will often follow up after reading the meeting notes.

Likely you've heard the term "death by slideshow" before. It's a chronic misuse of powerful presentation software, and it's a plague on offices around the world. In general, it's caused by confusing graphics, too much text on each slide, and presenters reading every word they've typed instead of preparing a proper speech. The end result is that, hours later, you miss the goal.

The incoming workforce wasn't raised with meetings. They were raised with instant gratification. Facebook. YouTube. Google. Information is always just a click away. They bring that same attitude to work because they want to make an impact. They are passionate and driven. So when they're stuffed into a room for an hour-long presentation that could have been a five-minute email, it kills their motivation.

Now, that may seem to imply I'm only talking about millennials. I don't want to give the impression that only the younger generation hates meetings. They are frustrating, and often it's because the information is important. Slide decks can quickly and efficiently share an idea. It's the difference between collaboration and confusion. If you're spending hours on a slide deck with eight-point font, you're not effectively communicating with your team. That's time that could be better spent making an impact.

Consider the bottom line. Bain & Company studied large corporation time budgeting and found that a weekly mid-level manager meeting cost one organization over $15 million each year. That's just one meeting a week.[20]

Although the meetings you attend may not cost that much, they do represent cost. For example, each one-hour meeting with a five-person team making an average of $100,000 per year costs $350. If the team averages fifteen hours of meetings each week, the weekly cost of meetings is $5,250.

That's $273,000 annually for just five people. Imagine when you multiply that out for your entire company. For a one hundred-person company, that's $5.5 million annually. To continue a work habit that kills progress toward meaningful change. It makes no sense.

---

20 Michael Mankins, Chris Brahm, and Greg Caimi, "Your Scarcest Resource," *Harvard Business Review*, May 2014, https://hbr.org/2014/05/your-scarcest-resource.

Finding a way to reduce the number and/or length of meetings can provide a huge savings to your company. Curious how much? The *Harvard Business Review* has a great cost calculator that can help you quickly put a price tag on your time. From where I'm sitting, the value of that investment isn't there.

It's not just that these meetings are wasteful. They're expanding. In 1960, executives lost ten hours a week to meetings. Now it's closer to twenty-three hours. How is that possible? Sure, in 1960 it was easier to gather ten people into one room to get the word out. Nowadays I can do the same thing in five minutes with a single email. Hell, I could text my managers and be sure they saw the message in seconds. Why should I waste an hour of my time and theirs when this technology exists?

Meetings tend to be pretty shallow, even with agendas. There are no deep conversations or learning. Most devolve into pre-meetings for a future meeting about a specific topic. Then, when an actual important meeting rolls around, you've added so much fluff to it that the message is completely lost.

Elon Musk sent out tips to his Tesla employees on productivity. This list weighed heavily on the side of limited meetings. Some of his suggestions for reducing the time spent in meetings include the following:

- Leave meetings in which you cannot add value.

- Don't use vocabulary and acronyms that make communication difficult.

- Don't use the chain of command for communication—use the shortest path.

- Enable free flow of information between levels and departments.

- Use common sense, especially if a company rule doesn't apply to your particular situation.

Satya Nadella also thought about how people spend their time. In a recent *Freakonomics* podcast interview, he shared, "When I set up a review, it turns out that people will do at least five reviews before they show up to me because that's kind of how it goes, right? They review with their manager, or their manager will review with their manager. Depending on the topic and the matrix organization, it could become an exponential growth thing." Satya boiled his rules for efficient meetings down to three points:[21]

---

21 Justin Bariso, "Microsoft's CEO Knows How to Run a Meeting. Here's How He Does It," *Inc. com*, https://www.inc.com/justin-bariso/microsofts-ceo-knows-how-to-run-a-meeting-heres-how-he-does-it.html.

- Talk less

- Listen more

- Be decisive when the time comes

Meetings are just one symptom of the Busy Trap, but they're rooted in an old-fashioned mindset. Our bosses went to meetings, and their bosses went to meetings, and so on, so the pattern continues. Again, it's not that all gatherings of employees are bad, but you have to come in focused and understand how to collaborate.

Living the Gig Mindset changed the way I collaborate with others. When I first started engaging with free-lancers on projects, I'd ask them to set aside time for a conference call. What is a conference call? It's a meeting.

I remember reaching out to one freelancer early on, when I was still experimenting with my methods. I gave her the specifics of the task and then asked if she had a few min-utes to hop on a call to discuss. She replied that I could just shoot her an email with the bullet points. "Be specific. What do you need? When do you need it? How do you want it formatted?" She was asking me to take time on my own, gather my thoughts together, and *then* provide instruction.

The freelancers in my network planned their days to maximize impact or reskilling. My twenty-minute phone call would throw the whole system off. Instead, I drafted a quick design brief that summarized my thoughts and needs. It took ten minutes and then one second to hit send on the email. Done.

Writing instructions down isn't just a benefit to your freelancer. It's a great exercise for gathering your thoughts and thinking critically. It forces you to consider how to best communicate expectations.

Jeff Bezos, the founder and CEO of Amazon, said in an interview that he doesn't let executives do slideshow presentations. Instead, they draft six-page narrative memos with focused language. That same method goes into my interactions with my freelance network. I write down my expectations so they can be clearly communicated rather than talking it out over the phone.

By applying a Gig Mindset and thinking in terms of what information this freelancer needed to be able to accomplish this task, I learned different ways of capturing and communicating ideas: ways that enabled us to avoid a meeting, be respectful of each other's time, and make faster progress.

Here are five tasks I have put into practice as I have worked to reclaim time and reinvent the way I work:

1. **Confirm we need structured time.** I will spend time working with the team to decide if we really need a meeting. Before setting up a meeting, I will always ask if the structured time is really needed and if there is a better way to accomplish the desired outcome. As I put the Gig Mindset into practice, I find myself breaking goals down into smaller tasks. This taskification doesn't lend itself to monolithic meetings. I will do everything in my power to avoid pulling people into a meeting room. If we absolutely have to meet, I'll limit it to thirty minutes with a solid agenda and clear outcome. I'll follow two pieces of advice from Jeff Bezos: the two pizza rule (meetings shouldn't be so big that two pizzas wouldn't feed everyone in the room) and no end-of-day meetings (10 a.m. is the magical time).

2. **Work in the open.** I will focus on increasing transparency by working in the open. This will create more fluid conversations, enable faster innovation, and produce better-quality projects. I will also do this by moving *all* of my project-based work to Slack or Microsoft Teams to ensure that all communication is transparent and in the open. We will leverage collaboration tools to form ideas and write our plans down *before* proposing a structured meeting. While the goal is to increase the pace of innovation and empower the team, it will also serve to reduce the need for as many structured meetings.

3. **Embrace the modern watercooler.** I will spend more time on spontaneous conversations about important projects, personal passions, and items that may seem random but often unlock innovation. Over time I will work to move some of these conversations on Slack or Microsoft Teams to drive engagement in the conversation. I will increase my engagement with other thought leaders on LinkedIn, which has increasingly become a virtual meeting place for conversation. I will encourage more productive conversations by moving strategy discussions out of the settings where operational work is performed. It's critical for me to ensure I get a diversity of thought and interaction from people "outside of the bubble." In my experience, taking a walk or grabbing coffee to discuss strategy leads to more productive and active conversations, which then helps push concepts forward without more formal meetings.

4. **Write things down.** I will take time to deeply think through my ideas and write them down as we work to make progress on various strategies and projects. I'm impressed with Amazon's approach that requires teams to write six-page narrative papers that outline new business innovation and current business challenges. It requires deep thinking and forces team collaboration and consensus. And there are *no slides!* The number of times I've pinged someone for info

and been told "it would be easier to get on a call" is insane. Ever since my freelancer set me straight, I've spent more time really working to understand and structure my thinking. Writing your thoughts down helps clear your mind and clarify your goals, priorities, and intentions.

5. **Learn to say "no."** Due to my insatiable curiosity, the hardest thing for me to do is say no. This is partly for FOMO—fear of missing out—and partly due to my belief that I may be missing a learning opportunity. I will be more deliberate with my time and work with colleagues to really understand where I can provide value to any meeting. I will also decline meetings where I cannot provide value.

The data is telling us to change, our leaders are pushing us to change, and we want change. These are my commitments to improving the efficiency of my time and respecting the time of those around me. Time is the most precious nonrenewable resource we have, and I want to ensure that it is spent in pursuit of empowering others, refreshing myself, and achieving more personally and professionally.

Cutting meetings out of your life creates time and space to do other tasks, like reskilling in order to stay current.

Paul: Resetting defaults is about changing with the times, and few people know that as well as John Winsor. He's worked in numerous industries and seen firsthand the rapid effects of the Gig Economy.

John: That's true, Paul. I spent decades in advertising, and the Gig Economy forced the industry to adapt and overcome. It may not have been on a personal level, but advertisers had to learn to reset their defaults.

I'm just in awe of the way that digital technology has empowered gig workers to be micro-entrepreneurs. One of my favorites is my buddy, Jimmy Chin.

Jimmy was known in the climbing community as a "dirtbag climber"—intentionally living cheap so he could spend his money on climbing. He was a Nat Geo photographer, and he made a couple movies. He got married to a filmmaker. And three years later, he won an Oscar for the long-form documentary for *Free Solo*. He's been a climbing partner for a long time. I look at his journey, he went from 14,000 Instagram followers in three years to three million. And I look at the way that information used to go out.

The way the information used to happen would be: Jimmy wins the Oscar; *Outside* magazine says, "Oh." The editor of *Outside* says, "Oh, that's cool. Let's find Jimmy, let's send a team of writers and photographers out to do an article on him." That takes a couple of months, *Outside* says, "Let's film that, let's produce it. Let's put it on this page of the magazine. Let's print it." That takes a couple more months. Finally the editor says, "As we go to press, we'll get Jaguar Land Rover Ltd to run an ad next to the article, and they'll pay $150,000 for the ad."

Outside has 650,000 readers of their magazine. They also have 800,000 followers on Instagram. The way it works now is that Jaguar Land Rover Ltd sees that Jimmy won an Oscar, calls Jimmy, or direct messages him on Instagram.

"Hey, Jimmy, will you do something with us? A little viral marketing?"

Jimmy says, "Yeah, show up in Jackson Hole with a car. And I'll do you two posts on Instagram of photos that I took with your car for $50,000." And it happens in two days. So, all those people—those tens of people that came up with a strategy for the story and wrote the story and photographed the story, and sold the advertising and printed the magazine, that whole set of intermediaries are just gone. The brand Jaguar Land Rover Ltd has called Jimmy; Jimmy takes two photos. And the next day just puts it up on Instagram and three million people see it.

Not only is it more efficient, from a cost perspective, it's way better from a marketing perspective too. It's way more authentic. It touches way more readers, or way more fans. And it's a better system. So I think we've seen that in all walks of life. And what we see—and what I see in the marketing-advertising business—is that if you're in those incumbent organizations, it's such a mind shift you can't even understand it.

Paul is talking about a mindset shift, and that excites me. That's what is so important here.

I was on the phone the other day with a guy from Columbia, and we were talking about whether or not the Gig Economy will take off, and what's hindering it. He pointed to a really interesting statistic. "Currently, there are 215,000 cell phone towers in the United States. And the big cell companies have just thousands of people to put towers up and work on maintaining that stuff. With 5G coming, there will be 5.5 million cell phone towers. There's no way that companies can hire enough full-time employees to put all those cell phone towers up."

So what's going to happen is it's going to be all driven by freelance workers. You'll sign on to a site and say, "I want to put some towers up and get certified." Then you'll run around, putting up micro towers piece by piece. And when they go online, you'll get paid. That's an inevitability. Those who build these new skills that Paul talks about will be the winners.

THE HANDYMAN AND THE HOUSE

If you're trying to adopt the Gig Mindset, you can't just dive in without any practice. That means learning how to taskify, how to delegate properly, and all of the underlying skills you don't even know you need.

First of all, take a deep breath. When I first started this, I had no idea what I was doing either. In fact, that's a great point to keep in mind.

Think of any person you admire from any profession. They could be an athlete, a creative type, an entrepreneur. Doesn't matter. Picture them in your mind. What is it about them that inspires you? That they are so talented, so effortlessly gifted, so accomplished?

Now remember that, at some point in their lives, they were none of those things. At one point in Stephen King's life, he had never written a single story. It took a long time before he sold even one. Tim Ferriss wasn't an overnight success. Bill Gates had to struggle to emerge from a suddenly crowded industry.

When we think of these people, we tend to focus on their

current states of success. We forget to take the time to understand their journeys. There was a great article on Business Insider that took a look at sixteen people who worked incredibly hard to succeeded: Venus and Serena Williams were up hitting tennis balls at 6 a.m. from the time they were seven and eight years old; Pepsi CEO Indra Nooyi worked the graveyard shift as a receptionist while putting herself through Yale; and Mark Cuban didn't take a vacation for seven years while starting his first business.[22]

There aren't a lot of stories about the late nights and early mornings that these "overnight successes" put in, grinding for new skills until they could barely stand. Basically, I'm saying don't give up when you aren't perfect right away.

When I started with the Gig Mindset, I worried about this too. I was up at 3 a.m. every morning, trying out new tasks and new projects. If you flip to the end of this book, you'll see one hundred tasks I was able to do by engaging with freelancers. That took time and practice. It took early mornings and late nights. I had to change the way I lived and worked. Now, you might read this paragraph and feel

---

22   https://www.businessinsider.com/16-people-who-worked-incredibly-hard-to-succeed-2012-
      9#dallas-mavericks-owner-mark-cuban-didnt-take-a-vacation-for-seven-years-while-starting-
      -his-first-business-3.

somewhat apprehensive. It sounds daunting. But I did all of that so that you wouldn't have to.

In order to succeed, you have to be willing to fail. That means you need to experiment, to learn by doing.

A lot of big corporations train people with videos or lectures. We get this picture in our heads that learning a new skill means a big classroom and a written test. If we don't have some certified, bona fide expert shouting acronyms and buzzwords, we must not be making progress.

You learn every single day; it's just not noticeable. You learn a faster route to work, you learn about preparing your meals better, you learn which songs you like or don't like. You learn by doing. Why couldn't you do the same for bigger skills? As Bill Gates famously said, "People overestimate what they can do in a day, and underestimate what they can do in a lifetime."

Another way to talk about this is the handyman and the house. When I talk about resetting your defaults, I'm talking about the way you approach growth in your industry and your company. I'm talking about the way you learn, the way you evolve. I'm talking about redefining your comfort zone.

Imagine a handyman tasked with building a house. On his own, he's very capable. He can fix plumbing, touch up the walls, and paint the rooms. His task, however, is too big for him to do alone. It's overwhelming. A whole house?

Now imagine he has a deadline approaching. How is he going to be able to accomplish his task when there is only so much time in the day? He'll need to engage with contractors. He needs to find experts to help tackle the various tasks.

This is where the T.I.D.E. model comes in. Our handyman has a large task to accomplish, and he's going to succeed by using these simple steps.

First, he breaks down the process of building a house into tasks. He has to lay a foundation, set up walls, build the support structure, lay the pipes and wiring, install fixtures, and eventually paint and set a roof on top. I'm sure we could break it down even more, but you get the idea.

Second, he identifies what he has to do, what he can drop, what gets delayed for later, and what he'll delegate to an expert. Like you, the handyman wants to work. He wants to have an impact on this important project. Since he can't do everything, he brings in contractors from various trades to take on the expert-level tasks.

Third, he delegates the work. Every contractor brought in has specific guidance on what they are doing, how it fits in, and when they need to be done. Everyone works off the same plan so they know the handyman's intent. There's no need to constantly meet and decide since everyone starts on the same page.

Fourth, he evolves his process, reviewing and improving where he needs. He's no longer just a handyman. He has learned project management and is now a contractor who can build a house.

Got it?

Could the handyman have done the job on his own? It's possible. It would have meant many more days of work for him, less time at home with his family, and the added stress all that would bring. He would have surrendered to the Busy Trap.

With the Gig Mindset, he identified the network needed to tackle this large project. Engaging with a freelancer enabled him to scale his own abilities and create more space in his life.

The handyman didn't change. His goal didn't change. All that he did was change the way he thought about the job.

A key to building a successful toolbox is experimentation, so it's time to go to the lab.

THE WORLD IS YOUR LAB; EXPERIMENT TO WIN

When I first started living the Gig Mindset, I picked my passion projects. I wanted something to do with my daughters, and that led to the strawberry festival. I wanted tickets to a cool concert. I wanted a flight for a vacation. It got me thinking: if the Gig Economy can change the way I live, it can change the way I work. If I use the same services and techniques around the office, what would that do to my productivity?

That's a great way to start. We're comfortable engaging with freelancers for our home life because we've been doing it for so long. You'd hardly notice the difference between ordering a pizza and ordering pizza from Postmates. Those are easy one-and-done tasks. The next step is arranging a project.

Projects require a bit more planning on your part. Again, start small. Look at the back of this book, and you'll find one hundred tasks I've completed to give you some inspiration on where you can start. I went from running scared to thinking there was light at the end of the tunnel, and it didn't take a leap of faith. It took the willingness to experiment.

That's why you start small. Pick a project with low stakes. Experiment. Fail. Learn. Improve. As you get more comfortable and confident with your network, your projects will scale as well. You'll learn how to provide specific instructions and clearer communication of your expectations. This will in turn help your freelancers provide you with better and better end results.

Maybe you've got work handled, or you're not able to share your workload outside of the company (for security or proprietary reasons). There are numerous projects in your life that could use a rework with the Gig Mindset. You can engage with freelancers to research that idea for a startup, help you with nonprofit work, or manage your side hustle. There could be an idea you've had in the back of your head that has never seen the light of day, and you just want someone to vet it.

Harvard Business Review wrote an article in 2017 stating that everyone, even executives, needs that side hustle.[23] It used to be that "moonlighting" was a bad word, a sign that you weren't taking your job seriously. Now it's almost expected that you'll use your free time to learn new skills, expand your horizons and network, and prepare for an uncertain future.

It's time to put your mindset to work. Enough worry and enough waiting. Roll up your sleeves, pick a project, and

---

23   Dorie Clark, "Even Senior Executives Need a Side Hustle," *Harvard Business Review*, November 29, 2017, https://hbr.org/2017/11/even-senior-executives-need-a-side-hustle.

get to it. If you don't, there's only one way this ends; reskill or die.

RESKILL OR DIE

Okay, maybe "die" is too harsh. I can get a little passionate here. I've been living in and writing about the Gig Mindset for years. It's literally changed my life, and I've seen its effect on hundreds of others. This is real, this works, and it will work for you.

But you need to reskill. Your education is nearing its expiration date. Your expertise is less useful by the day. You need time and space to learn and grow so you can continue being the amazing person you are. I want you to succeed; that's why I'm pushing you so hard.

As Stephane Kasriel said, you need to take stock of the half-life of your skills. In his article, he pointed out that self-driving trucks are an inevitable disruption in the near future. If you're a truck driver, you need to be reskilling right now. Preparing for the future isn't just about the loss of a career either.

Look back to 2010. Jobs like social media manager or YouTube creator or app developer didn't exist. There have been 10 million applications created for iOS and Android alone. The Uber mobile app launched in 2011, and now there are 400,000 drivers in the US and over 110 million users worldwide. By 2025, there will be 100,000 drone operators in a wide variety of industries providing services we cannot even imagine today.

Those numbers should excite you. That's the future we can look forward to, and the relevant skills exist today. What you learn by engaging with the Gig Mindset will prepare you for the curves in the road ahead. According to the US Department of Labor, the average American spends only 4.2 years in a job before moving to the next one. Instead of worrying about how you'll make an impact, revel in the opportunities this variety can provide.

I remember living in that Busy Trap. I woke up super stressed every day. I'd try my best to spend time with my girls, but I usually just kissed them goodbye on my way out to another meeting. Or I had to get to work early to prepare for a meeting. I felt like I wasn't making progress, that the mountain of emails in my inbox never got any smaller. I just felt too busy.

I didn't have time to think. I didn't have the space to even come up with a plan of attack. Worse still, all my ideas had to be shelved so I could fight through the mountain of work piling up. I wanted to write a book about the Gig Economy, about the changes I saw happening in every industry, but where was the time? The more I thought about it, time spent on the idea could teach me how to work and live *better*. I could learn ways to help my company and our customers.

I remember sitting in my home office and looking out the window to a beautiful sunny day. I remember thinking, what will it be like when my daughters are grown? When they have sports. When I miss games because of presentation preparation, meetings, and an overall lack of time.

That's death. That's a little taste of death right there. And it's bitter.

You need to reskill. To reskill, you need space. To get space, you need to change something in your life. You need to reset your defaults.

I remember that moment in my office, sitting across from a single mother in need of a break. When she saw what the Gig Mindset could do for her, in just a few minutes, her eyes lit up. Her life changed in front of me. In an instant, she saw possibility. She saw space for herself.

It's time to make your own.

THE T.I.D.E. MODEL

"Many of our best opportunities were created out of necessity. "

—SAM WALTON, FOUNDER OF WALMART

Do you know the story of Henry Ford and the assembly line? It's fascinating. Even if you don't know all the details, you know the end result: The Ford Model T becomes cheaper and faster to produce, and it floods the market to become one of the best-selling cars in history. At the same time, Ford established the idea of a workplace as one location you worked at nine to five.

When we think of the Industrial Revolution, we often limit it to the new technology that emerged or the new industries that formed. It's rare that you hear someone lecturing about the incredible changes in mindset brought about by this epic shift in the world. The truth is that we wouldn't have had a revolution of any kind without serious changes in the way we think. Henry Ford looked at the status quo, at his defaults, and realized he needed to make a change.

It started with the Model N. Ford cranked out Model N cars at about two a day. He had his workers lay out the parts over a big blueprint and then assemble in a series of steps. That meant a lot of moving parts in and out of that small circle until the car was complete. Ford saw that as inefficient, so he had the entire vehicle put on sleds at one end of the line and dragged down to the other end. Now all the parts could be laid out along the path and added on as the vehicle passed.

Still, it took twelve hours to get through a single Model N. There were too many steps to remember, and the workers had to juggle various jobs. Ford broke down the process of assembling the new Model T into eighty-four specific steps; then he trained his workers to perform exactly one of those steps each. He created experts in those individual tasks.

Then he called in a motion-study expert, someone trained to visualize how objects and people can move more efficiently. The expert planned out the assembly process so that each step took as little time as possible. At the same time, Ford manufactured enormous machines to quickly stamp out parts for the Model T.

With a motorized line running at six feet per minute, the

Model T arrived fully formed in just two hours and thirty minutes. The assembly line was a revolution in and of itself, and it changed everything.

What Henry Ford accomplished sets the precedent for a modern reboot. We can learn everything we need about the Gig Mindset right here.

Up next, we're going to go over the T.I.D.E. Model. In it, various thought leaders and I will teach you how to taskify, identify, delegate, and evolve. This is a modern system for knowledge and digital work but also what Henry Ford went through to develop the assembly line.

First, he broke down the construction of the Model T in eighty-four steps. Think about it. If I asked you to build a car, you could do it. People build cars in their backyards all the time. You would most likely ask for instructions to help you along. What if I gave you a sheet of paper that just said: Step One—Build a Car?

Would you even know where to start?

Now, if I gave you an eighty-four-page booklet with a breakdown of steps, the goal would start to become more manageable. Like the old saying from General Creighton Abrams Jr., "When eating an elephant, take one bite at a time." You break down the process into simple steps, and suddenly the complex becomes clear. That's taskification.

After he had his steps, Henry had to identify his experts. He assigned his workforce their steps and brought in an expert to orchestrate the process. That efficiency of movement was what Ford needed to improve his process. That's what identification is all about. The proper engagement of experts and selecting the work that you want to do.

As we go forward, think about how you will evolve in this system.

Then, with all the pieces in place, Ford delegated the work. He didn't sit and watch a million Model T vehicles cross the line. He installed leadership, set expectations, and gave up control of the process. Once his expectations were set, he gave up control of the process. For many people, this is the most difficult part of the process. Delegation requires clear communication, guidance, and trust.

Finally, with everything moving forward, Henry Ford evolved. When his blueprint plan was too slow, he put the car on sleds. When that was too slow, he made an automatic track. When his machinists took too long to make the parts for each vehicle, he invented machines to stamp them out faster. He identified areas for improvement and made those improvements. Evolution is tricky, and it requires you to accept mistakes and learn from them.

It is about being open to continuous learning. Researcher Carol Dweck dubbed these the Growth and Fixed Mindsets. In a Fixed Mindset, the person believes their talent and intelligence is set, therefore they cannot change or grow beyond a set point. With a Growth Mindset, the person understands that their skills grow over time, so they can continually improve their capabilities with effort. When you combine this with the idea of evolution, you come to realize that your potential only stops when *you* stop moving.

In 1913, Henry Ford introduced the assembly line, and in 1924 he watched the 10 millionth Model T drive off the lot. His change in mindset enabled him and his company to rise above the competition and remain relevant, creating an impact still felt to this day. He threw away the old script, invented a new model, and taught his team how to succeed.

Now, I'm going to do the same with you.

T.I.D.E. MODEL

Everyone has a list of tasks they want to do. A friend of mine calls it her "Should List." It's all those things we "should" do, if only we had the time and space to do them. "Should" became a bad word in her household. It was shorthand for "this will never get done." So she flipped the mentality. She got out a whiteboard and wrote down her Should List, noting all the chores they wanted to get done around the house, as a family and individually. Then she crossed out the word "should" and put "I will."

Changing your mindset is the first step. Turning a task from something you'll get to "one day" into a project you'll start "today" takes a flip of a switch. Making time to actually action those tasks takes a little more. She gave each of those should tasks a deadline. If she couldn't take care of it on her own, or her family couldn't make time, then it was freelanced out. Her mentality was that the task *would* get done, and it didn't necessarily have to be by her.

I discovered that engaging with freelancers on simple tasks opened up space in my life to focus on my own Should List.

I remember the first year of the Gig Mindset. I was like a kid with a new toy. Every morning I would wake up, head downstairs, and start up new projects. Engaging with freelancers energized me. I started creating new content, articles, and websites and delegating my daily to-do list. I learned how to speak the language, how to quickly describe what I wanted, and how to find the right people for the project.

One day I decided I wanted to start a podcast. Before, I would have had no idea where to start. The sheer scope of it would have scared me off. I realized that, while I could visualize my goal, I was looking at it as one enormous leap. Step one was "Make a Podcast." That's impossible. It's the same as saying step one is "Build a Car."

Rather than get discouraged, I used my new superpower. I asked the experts. On one site—Clarity.fm—I found someone who was an expert in creating podcasts, and they saved me hours of online research on everything from the equipment to the process. On another, I found some writers who could help with scripts for each episode. On a third, I engaged with sound editors to edit the interviews. In just weeks, I had a team of people helping me design my project.

What may be lost in that last paragraph is just how much time I saved. Before, I would have spent a few hours searching around the internet. I would have typed in some key phrases, hopefully found the right sites, and tried to teach myself a whole list of new skills. That doesn't even touch the time to research topics, write scripts, learn new software, and find plenty of hardware for the audio engineering side.

It took some trial and error, but I started identifying efficiencies. Like Ford watching over his automotive plant, I saw the points of friction in my new network of experts. Over time, my podcast turned into my own little assembly line. I had the help I needed to achieve my goal and the space needed to focus on my own areas.

The idea started to click for me, and after a few months I had the foundation of a system for this new mindset. I took care of everything from booking flights to research for presentations all through various online freelance marketplaces. I built a network of known and trusted freelancers, and I kept a running list of sites that provided useful tools and experts. In time, we started to trust each other, to know to efficiently work together. And we were able to do it without sitting around a table yawning through a slideshow presentation.

The more projects I did, the more my process improved, and the more my mindset solidified. Even though I was actually adding to my daily output, I found I had more time left for myself. By engaging with the Gig Economy, I had reclaimed my time. I could have a full day with my creative team, run side projects and experiment with my mindset, and still make time for my family. Years of practice were paying off.

Soon, my new lifestyle had a name: the Gig Mindset. I

knew what I was doing and how I wanted to do it. With each day, I refined my process, and suddenly I had honed it into four easy steps. Well, I shouldn't say easy. I should say easy-to-follow. As the plaque on President Obama's desk read, hard things are hard. If you want to follow my mindset, to understand my process, you need to be ready for the hard work it takes.

Lucky for you, I've done a lot of the legwork. What I discovered, waking up early in the morning to start new projects, was a four-step method to success.

I didn't even realize I had the process until a colleague of mine asked me to speak to his class. I'd been living this new lifestyle, this new mindset, and he wanted me to share with his students the work I was doing. I'd never sat down to think about how I could actually teach someone this process. How could I make an exercise for the class where it would actually find value?

I started writing on my whiteboard. I posted up pictures and drew lines connecting the different ideas. I must have looked like a crazy person; it was like that scene from *A Beautiful Mind*. It all snapped together, it synthesized, and I realized there was a simple model sitting right in front of me. Something I had been doing without even knowing. The T.I.D.E. Model: Taskify, Identify, Delegate, and Evolve.

TASKIFICATION

Henry Ford broke down the process of building a Model T into eighty-four steps. Each one of those steps required a very specific action, and Ford turned a single employee into an expert for each of those steps. You have to do the same.

More importantly, you have to become goal oriented. This model is all about outcomes. Start with something small, something you know well. Maybe you want a fun day out with family. That's a fairly simple request. If you had all the time in the world, it might only cost you a few hours to plan it out.

Look, life is made up of tasks. You don't just get ready for work. You get out of bed, you brush your teeth, you take a shower, you get dressed, you make breakfast, and you drive to work. All of those are discrete and individual tasks.

It's the same with work. Presentations don't create themselves. They start with research, and then you make an outline, and then you get data and graphs. You get updates from people that are doing various projects, and you synthesize the feedback. All of these are individual tasks that lead to a final outcome.

I realized that if I wanted to launch a website, there were

five or six or seven tasks within that goal: there's over-all site design, content, site administration, data input, coding, front end and back end, articles to write, etc. All of these tasks could be handed off to one person, but then I'm not gaining any time. More to the point, I'm not getting the best product, since I'm expecting one person to be an expert in all these fields.

Taskification is taking that goal and turning it into a series of steps. Specifically, you want to break down the task into expert-level parts. Henry Ford separated the assembly of the wheels and axles from the team installing seats and mirrors. In the same way, the person researching your restaurant might not be able to find the best activities.

In a business sense, the person who can design your website might not know as much about researching how to generate the best ad revenue on that site, or comparing you with competition, or search engine optimization.

Understanding your end goal helps you refine your taskification.

When I started out, I picked small projects. I needed to schedule my annual checkup, so I had a freelancer book the appointment. I needed some work done around the house, so I had that assistant research local handymen. When I tackled a big presentation at work, I created a network of researchers and designers to create powerful and persuasive slides. I grew more confident in the process and my results. The effect was like a snowball rolling down a hill.

As my process improved, I wanted to try more complex tasks. I decided to focus on building up my podcast, so I worked with Clarity.fm and other sites to research exciting topics. With those bullet points in hand, I was able to deliver engaging content for my listeners. With another freelancer, I was able to find the best places to push that content and find my audience.

Freelancers can take my notes and transcriptions from talks I give and produce content that can be shared on social media. They do research, find images, and edit the content to fit my voice and style. They can look at my schedule and get my family tickets to a Dave Matthews concert. They can send me recipes based on what my daughters like to eat and what we have left in the refrigerator. Five minutes of issuing out a task gets me hours of work. That's a value that cannot be understated.

Taskification also ties into one of our previous topics: death to meetings. Breaking down your goals into tasks forces you to think in concise, simple instructions. You're building the car piece by piece, so complexity is your enemy. This is doubly true in communication. With modern "watercoolers" like Slack and Microsoft Teams, you can take time to plan your collaboration in detail, link to files, and share your work in real time.

The mechanics building the Model T hadn't been manufacturing cars for decades. This was all still very new to the workforce, so Henry Ford had to break everything down into simple terms. In the same sense, you need to learn to speak clearly and concisely to your freelance teams. Don't overload them with buzzwords and jargon. Tell them what you need and what you expect for their tasks. Give them guardrails so they know where to start and when to end.

Taskification is also a measure of control. When you first start living the Gig Mindset, it's easy to fall back into old habits. You'll worry about your new team, about projects getting dropped, about jumping in too deep too early. Watching each task be completed grants you a little peace of mind. They're breadcrumbs your team can follow all the way to your goal.

It's important to practice taskification. So important, in fact, I'm dedicating an entire chapter to the topic with thought leaders from a variety of fields. We'll get to that in a few pages.

Once you've got a goal in mind, and you've broken it down into specific tasks, it's time to find your team.

IDENTIFICATION

Experts are not hard to come by in the Gig Economy. In fact, in my experience, there is a surplus ready to engage with those in need. They can be found with just a few minutes of searching online, and they are available to help you out in a number of ways. The freelancers in my network come from a variety of disciplines, all experts in their own fields. I have people I trust for planning, development, writing, design, market research, and for video. I know where to go and who to go to for my daily tasks, and that's invaluable.

Identification is crucial in finding the right expert for the right project. You need to have a job description, daily tasks, and candidates with the right match of attributes to come on board.

The difference is all about scope. When you hire a full-time employee, you have a laundry list of tasks that they'll need to do. In effect, you need a jack-of-all-trades. It's very different working with freelancers. You only need them to be an expert in the *one* task you've specified.

That's why taskification is the first step. If you don't know what you need done, and how it's broken into separate parts, you can't properly identify the right talent. Once you know exactly what you want, you can find an expert who has perfected performing that one specific task.

This also means that you need to let your freelancers stay in their Zone of Genius. A full-time employee can be asked to go a little outside their role. Most job descriptions have a line about "any other work as needed" at the bottom of the page. That's fine for internal workers, but not freelance experts. If they say they can do A and B, don't ask them for C. You're not hiring a plumber to fix your TV.

Identification also means locating and providing access to the necessary resources. Since freelancers aren't a part of your organization, you have to provide them the context on your culture, as you can't provide them with specific software.

Freelancers are doers, bringing in an entrepreneurial spirit that augments and invigorates projects. It brings a level of energy to a project that elevates the entire team. However, it would be too easy to overtask these freelancers and lose valuable time. That's why providing clear instructions and setting expectations are so important.

If you're engaging with freelancers for individual tasks, it's easy to identify the boundaries of work. When you are incorporating them into an active team, you have to be very specific about their area of control. So how can you be sure that the people you've selected are right for the task?

Almost every site you go to will include a portfolio of work for your potential freelancers. Most freelancers run a personal website as well to show off what they've done. That's a huge benefit to you when selecting your team.

Imagine calling in an applicant for a full-time position. Aside from their resumé, what would you have available to inform your decision? An interview can tell you a bit about culture fit, but what about their actual output? It's a gamble.

With freelancers, they don't leave anything to chance. They can't. They'll often have websites, references, ratings, online feedback, and anything else you'll need to make the most informed decision. They want the engagement to be positive. At the end of each job they get rated, and those comments are there for the next client to see. Imagine if that happened at your workplace. How much more energy would you put into each and every task?

Building your network of freelancers, just like everything else, requires time and experimentation. I engaged with hundreds of freelancers before I settled on my current network. Even now, I'll reach out to new freelancers just to see if a fresh eye can enhance my projects. It lets me test new ideas and easily tap into diversity of thought.

A friend works in real estate planning in the Midwest. He

wanted to research the Gig Economy and the impact on the future of work as it relates to the physical working environment. Before, he would have hired a consulting firm to gather that information. It would cost tons of money, take forever, and possibly not deliver the bullet points he needed to present the information to the broader team.

Instead, my colleague engaged three or four experts to research this topic for a short amount of time. These freelancers knew the subject matter well enough to focus their efforts. This meant it took less time, which means less expense overall. He was able to give a great presentation to the leadership team that was greatly supported by the evidence and underlying research. Most important of all, they achieved their outcome. That's what this process is all about: accomplishing your goals with the least friction.

Hard things are hard. Don't expect to be great at identifying the right talent right away. Work at it, experiment, and trust your instincts. Once you have broken down your tasks and identified your team, it's time to put them to work.

DELEGATION

This is the most challenging part of the T.I.D.E. Model. I

want you to know that up front. Breaking down tasks into smaller chunks gets easier with practice. Identifying your experts is just experimentation. Delegating work is hard, and you need to know that going in.

There's a great story from Ryan CEO at CompuVision in Canada. His team came down one week to pitch a significant sales opportunity. Millions of dollars were at stake.

It was a Monday, and the big meeting was on a Friday. His team set up time to review the pitch slides, and they were all over the place and lacked professional polish. The team had cobbled together slides from other presentations and then tried its best to clean up this Frankenstein monster.

Ryan knew he needed help, so he engaged a freelance designer to take the existing presentation and improve the flow and overall design. He gave specific instructions that he wanted professional visuals but also a more focused story all the way through. On Thursday, the deck came back from the freelancer, and the team was blown away.

Not only had the story improved, but it better represented the business and what it was trying to communicate. The team presented on Friday, confident and proud of what it was presenting. It had supplied all the information, but the freelancer translated that into something visually impressive. The CompuVision team won the business.

Ryan needed someone with expertise, and he didn't have them on his team. Fortunately, he was confident in engaging with a freelance designer. With the right amount of control and communication, he received exactly what he needed. Since that experience, Ryan has implemented freelancers across his business, and he encourages others to adopt this new way of working.

When you live the Gig Mindset, you become a leader. You collaborate with a small team and encourage its success. It's a strange feeling. If you're coming from a manager's perspective, it may seem familiar, but the reality of delegating to freelancers is something else entirely.

For one, you don't see your freelancer every day. Everything happens in real time. In a normal office environment, you can pop by and check on your employees. You can get a quick update on a project. You can offer small notes and corrections. You can—shudder—call a meeting.

Freelancers may work toward your deadlines, but they are on their own schedules. That's one of the main benefits of being a freelancer: no random meetings, no micromanagers, no office politics—jockeying for credit, getting the last word in, or just trying to be the smartest in the room. While that is great news for them, it can be a major pain point for you.

Delegation requires some skill to perform effectively. Namely, the following:

1. The ability to clearly communicate your end goals

2. Setting controls and milestones to judge progress

3. Establishing a simple system for reporting and checking in

4. Above all else, trust

Trust is the key. Trust is the difference between you reclaiming your time and you spending all your time stressed over this new project.

The first part is relatively easy. You've already broken down your tasks, you've identified this freelancer as your chosen expert, and now you've given them the word to begin. That's why I stressed being goal oriented. If you know what the end of the project should be, and you tell the rest of your team members, then they don't need to hear from you every single day.

Think about that handyman from a chapter back. If I tell him at the start, "I want this room painted blue," do I really need to check in on him every day? If I wasn't around, isn't my goal clear?

You need to communicate your goals just as clearly. Set the guidelines for success so your team can move forward without you. That's what reclaiming time really means: you don't even have to be there anymore for your vision to carry on.

Setting controls and milestones is another way to avoid micromanaging. Tell the handyman, "When you've finished two walls, send me an email." Now I can gauge the progress of this project without interrupting my freelancer or taking any additional time out of my day. It's an automatic process. It's like when you're installing new software, and the bar slowly fills up. There's a lot going on behind the scenes, but all you care about is how soon until it's complete.

However, none of this matters without trust. If you're a natural micromanager, trust can be hard to come by. As Kevin Plank, CEO of Under Armour, said, "Trust is gained in drops and lost in buckets." You don't know these freelancers personally, yet you're going to trust them with these important tasks?

Well, how much trust did you place in that Uber driver the other night? Or the Postmates delivery person? Or the virtual assistant booking your tickets to see your parents? Engaging with freelancers across the entire spectrum builds your confidence. Just like taskification and identification, this trust will build with use. It is earned as you do more and more projects. Building a durable and trusted network is key, and it doesn't happen overnight.

Rachel Botsman—a global thought leader on trust—gave a TED Talk that explained how the Gig Economy is a "Trust Economy."[24] She defines trust as a confident relationship to the unknown. In her talk, she explained how human beings are good at taking trust leaps, and that this is at the core of the rising Gig Economy. "Do you remember the first time you put your credit card details into a website? That's a trust leap. I distinctly remember telling my dad that I wanted to buy a navy blue, second-hand Peugeot on eBay, and he rightfully pointed out that the seller's name was Invisible Wizard and that this probably was not such a good idea."

Rachel believes this new paradigm will change our behaviors in the real world in ways we are just starting to understand. "I don't always bother to hang my towels up when I finished in the hotel, but I would never do this as a guest on Airbnb. The reason why I would never do this as a guest on Airbnb is because guests know that they'll be rated by hosts, and that those ratings are likely to impact their ability to transact in the future." Trust

---

24   Rachel Botsman, "The Currency of the New Economy is Trust." Filmed
      June 2012 at TEDGlobal, Video 19:32, https://www.ted.com/talks/
      rachel_botsman_the_currency_of_the_new_economy_is_trust?language=en.

is when you type in your credit card info to buy a used Beatles album on eBay. Trust is buying a few hours of a researcher's time for an important project. Trust is building a network to help with office projects. Once you start to trust in these freelancers, you'll be able to move forward with confidence.

Trust also helps dispel the myths around freelancers. People worry that they're unreliable, or their work quality is low, or they don't communicate well. I'm not going to say it's all roses. There are challenges. However, the positives I've experienced far outweigh the negatives. Freelancers deliver time and again on projects of all sizes.

Once you experiment enough, you'll find your rhythm in this new process. The Gig Mindset will be second nature. Then, when you've got some momentum, it's time to evolve.

EVOLUTION

Toyota has an impressive quality assurance model. For the longest time, I just enjoyed their vehicles. I drove a 4Runner for nineteen years and loved it. It got me looking into the company, trying to figure out what made them different than others in the automotive industry.

At Toyota factories, everyone is a quality assurance manager. Every person on the line can stop the process cold if they're concerned about quality. Consider the cost of shutting down the line for even an hour, and yet the company puts that amount of trust in their employees.

That kind of faith didn't happen overnight. Toyota grew with the times. They tried new processes, experimented, and made adjustments. They *evolved*.

In the same way, I've come to view my freelance team as collaborators. When we're on a project, any one of them can raise a red flag if they have concerns about quality. They can make suggestions, push back, and take some ownership of the final product. That didn't happen right out of the gate. I had to learn and grow myself.

I had to create an environment where I *wanted* the feedback from experts. They pushed to make their process better, so I had to ensure they were encouraged from the start to provide feedback and ideas. After all, what's the point of engaging with experts if you don't treat them as such?

All these big ideas led to new research, which led to new ideas. It was a wild cycle. To keep up, I started engaging with researchers, having them do the legwork on gathering information and condensing it into digestible chunks. Pro designers built presentations that focused all that research into persuasive arguments. Editors cleaned up the language so that everything flowed toward a shared outcome. That freed me up to combine these ideas, think bigger, and grow faster.

That's when I realized: I wasn't the pilot anymore. I was the air traffic controller. I was the conductor of an orchestra, a creative director running a team of artists. I was in the flow.

This is a radical change. It's rethinking what's possible. It's exponential growth in your overall productivity. And it all starts with that very simple mentality. You're not the person flying the plane. You control pilots across multiple disciplines, and you're ushering ideas from one stage of development to the other.

That realization is the reason you're holding this book right now. This evolution changed my life. You don't have to be an expert in everything; you just need to bring them to you.

Yes, you need the idea, the seed that's going to grow into something real. You have to be goal oriented. You must understand the tasks involved, select your experts, and delegate responsibility. But then you can let these incredible freelancers bring your idea to reality. There is nothing preventing you from finishing that "Should List." Your passion project can be achieved!

How many times have you been at dinner with friends, heard something, and said, "I had that idea a year ago. I never knew what to do with it?"

The difference between having an idea and delivering value is execution. If it's in your head, it can easily be brought to reality. That's the Gig Mindset. That's what this model can do.

Standing up a new website and building a team of experts is less expensive than even just a few years ago. Before, you needed to be inside a company and convince the entire organization to make any movement. You needed the infrastructure, the talent pool, the financing. You needed to hire an HR recruiter before you could even start looking for your team! Now, you can go directly to the experts. This takes far less time and is far more efficient, and you'll have more control over the results.

Now, with very little budget, I was able to move fast and keep energy around my new ideas. My rapid experimentation led to innovation in the process and helped me build trust with a growing network of experts. I reskilled along the way, learning while doing.

I'm fortunate that big companies are starting to embrace this idea. They're starting to say, "How can we move faster? How do we enable the intelligence of our mission-focused employees to unlock what's possible for our customers?" If a big ship can turn this direction, there are no obstacles for you or your company to do the same.

The T.I.D.E. Model, my blueprint for the Gig Mindset, is deceptively simple. Four easy steps. Anyone can do it. Yet to be successful, you need to work at this every day. This is your new normal. There is a reason I insisted you reset your defaults before we got here. Can you imagine the old you trying any of this?

Thomas Friedman, a Pulitzer Prize-winning journalist, wrote the book *The World Is Flat*. He said that cheap connectivity in hardware is flattening the global playing field. In the past, engaging a company in India—or even just across the country—required attending an in-person meeting and signing a huge contract. In contrast, my gig team is all over the world.

The next few chapters are where the rubber meets the road. I've assembled a panel of experts, CEOs, and thought leaders. I am incredibly grateful to have their stories and guidance to share with all of you. It's time for you to channel your inner Henry Ford. Visualize that assembly line and start breaking it down, task by task. It's time to put the model to the test.

TASKIFY

"You don't have to be a genius or a visionary or even a college graduate to be successful. You just need a framework and a dream."

—MICHAEL DELL

Let me tell you about my week. I had my virtual assistant set up my annual physical. They booked me an appointment for my eye doctor. I'm having the sprinklers turned on at my house, and they set that up. I wanted to see a Dave Matthews concert with my family, so they cross-referenced my calendar, found tickets, and purchased them.

I had a water leak not long ago, and my virtual assistant contacted the Water District to figure it all out. When my air conditioner failed, they researched HVAC companies to get quotes, selected the best one, and booked it. When I needed to pitch a new idea to the executive team, I used my network to research and design a powerful presentation. When I had a great interview to post on LinkedIn, I had professional writers and editors to help create compelling articles.

This is what taskification has done for me: I rarely talk on the phone anymore. When I have to spend time calling folks, or waiting for them to call me, it feels weird. Alien. I've had 465 calls made on my behalf in the past eighteen months.

All my dinner reservations, all my house projects, even moss removal around my house—I have a virtual assistant to take care of it all.

Taskification can be big and it can be small. Everything I just listed falls under "home chores" and "personal needs." Nonstop goals. I know I'm going to need a doctor visit every year. I know I'm going to need my house maintained. These are tasks I can do myself, but those hours could be better spent on bigger projects. There's not a lot of heavy lifting, just a lot of time spent. There is also a great return on investment. When I needed a remodel done, my virtual assistant researched multiple quotes and saved over 50 percent on the project, which more than paid for the cost of the service for multiple years.

These are just some examples that worked for me. You

might enjoy taking a hands-on approach to home repair, and that's great. Just imagine how many more projects you could tackle by engaging with experts on the tasks you *don't* enjoy?

In the previous chapter, we looked at the general idea of taskification. In theory, it's all very simple. You have an idea, a goal, a mission. You break it down into digestible steps and specified tasks and get to work.

We're not trying to just build a car. We're stamping sheet metal, attaching wheels, connecting the doors. Small steps lead to the big product.

As an example, I cover a number of topics in my writing and on my podcasts. I remember a meeting at work where we started to discuss incubation projects. They're a fascinating topic, and I wanted to become super smart about them. I needed to be an expert if I was going to write articles, talk to guests, and bring that energy into work. In the past, I would have tooled around the internet, clicking on whatever site had the best SEO. Now, I reached out to actual experts in the field and gave them the task of bringing me up to speed.

Six hours later, I had pages of notes, suggestions for podcasts, and a strong foundation for becoming a subject-matter expert.

The best way to learn this method is to actually practice. Pick something you want to learn, or something you *need* to learn, and task out a freelancer to find you the answers. This is the first task, and it will spawn numerous others.

Taskification is also about recognizing your abilities—and your limitations. I'm not a designer. That's not humility; I really can't design. If you hired me for my artistic sensibilities, then I'm sorry. That was poor judgment on your part. However, in my work I need great design for products and presentations. When you look at what I'm producing on LinkedIn, or Twitter, or exploring product innovation, you'll see plenty of design work that is top-notch. All of that came from engaging with expert and talented freelancers.

Let's break down a simple task: a thought leadership article. My end goal, at the end of the next two paragraphs, is a LinkedIn article. Let's see how we can get it done.

I'm at a conference listening to a number of interesting speakers when one of the topics piques my interest. I go to the presenter—an entrepreneur or CEO or generally interesting person—and ask if they have twenty minutes to sit and talk. That's something I do often, just grab mini-interviews. I record the conversation on my phone. Afterward, I send that recording to a site for transcription and set a task for additional research with a virtual assistant to build out some more detail based on the conversation.

Once all my information is together, I send it to a writer who knows my tone and voice. (Side note: I actually had a freelancer create a voice tone document so that future freelancers have a template.)

I have another freelancer pulling images together that complement the story and another doing additional research on the topic. All the while, I form the goal and flow of the article before handing it off so my expectations are set.

I post up to LinkedIn to connect with a network of professionals as I help companies understand strategies to start engaging with freelancers. I spent twenty minutes talking to a speaker, maybe another twenty on typing out my tasks. Less than an hour of work and I have a completed article, fully researched, on LinkedIn. I had an outcome in mind, set my expectations, and got the results I wanted.

That's how easy taskification can be. It's about being goal oriented and then breaking down the steps.

But here I am hogging the pages. Let's ask our thought leaders how taskification works for them.

MIKE MORRIS

Paul: Mike, how do you approach taskification?

Mike: Everything at Topcoder is about taskification. Our system relies on breaking down goals into tasks.

Paul: So what lessons have you learned over the years that has made you more effective? What can readers take away?

Mike: I would say what it really comes down to is managing your time. In running a business, a lot of your time and energy is spent in the EQ part of your world: managing relationships, managing people. And we see that industries that are able to switch that pyramid around and make it run off more of your qualitative or IQ side of your brain can become so much more efficient. And that's one of the biggest benefits that we see in how our platform works; we're managing a process in a platform, we're not managing 1.4 million people.

I'm trying to say that we care tremendously about the 1.4 million people in our community, we care about the 1.4 million people in aggregate. So we very much make sure that when we're building a process, we're building a methodology, we are building it for scale and not to be single threaded between two particular individuals, and that has been a huge impact for us.

Now there's the downside of that. Myself and the majority of our team at Topcoder is today, and has traditionally been, from a technology background. We tend to over-complicate things very quickly and very easily.

So in the beginning, sometimes we'll get into a place where we become so fixated on the process—it should work like this, this, this, and that's automated, and this is measured, and that goes from here to here—and nobody touches it. And at the end of it we're like, "Ooh we just built a Rube Goldberg." Like the most complicated way possible to turn on a light.

You have to watch out for those things, we always have to watch out for those, but I would say that we've really changed. Uber doesn't manage all of their drivers, but they do manage a very strict process, and that's what we've done in our space.

A lot of what we found out was by design, and part was by luck. But one of the challenges that we realized as we were building our model, we found very quickly that people had very different skillsets. Some people were really good at algorithms, some people are really good at writing very strong code. Some people are really good at breaking code, some people are really good at the creative side of coding. And it was rare—very, very rare—to find one person who could do it all.

We have this role called a copilot, and the copilots in the Topcoder community must earn their way into this role by being a great competitor, by being an accomplished community member. They come in, they work on projects, they get their ratings and their statistics, and then we invite them to be a copilot.

They help to manage the work streams, so their primary job is being able to take a project and break it into its pieces: Taskification. Think of it like there's thirty different Lego block shapes that we can break our projects into.

That's a copilot's job. They take a piece of work and they say, "All right, well I need these ten steps in order to get this result." That's taskification.

Let's say we're building an iPad application and it has to have a front end that's intuitive and beautifully designed so that people want to use it. And it has to be interactive in a way that doesn't require typing, and the back end has to perform, it has to be well written, and run on a server, and all those things that a software project would need. All those different tasks.

So that copilot will then say, "All right, well the first problem I need is to figure out how this is going to work, so I need a wireframe. I need to get wireframes, so let me get five different versions of a wireframe so then I can find out which is the best." So he breaks it down and says, "All right, that's a piece that we need to get done. That's step one."

Well the same time he's figuring out that wireframe, he can also go run the front end design because he knows the end product needs to be intuitive and beautiful. He has the branding requirements and all that. "I know what the front page is gonna look like, so let me go run a really awesome design challenge and get a bunch of great designers to give me ideas. I can combine their collective creativity, create an amazing output, and that can happen at the same time."

Two tasks now running simultaneously. The copilot spends the same amount of time, but accomplishes twice as much. Makes sense?

The copilot just defined his requirements through those two taskified pieces of work. Then he can go in and say, "Well, now I need to taskify this into development tasks, I gotta get it built." He's already thinking a few steps ahead because the first few steps are automated. They're being done in the background.

Next, he has five sprints that have to get done. Five more steps. With the Topcoder platform, the copilot can engage five freelancers to start simultaneously and build. We can send them out to get built and they integrate right back into the main tree without ever having to worry about it. It's continuous integration: develop, integrate, develop, integrate, develop, integrate.

You do that five times and all of a sudden you now have a piece of code that looks great, that does what you need it to do, and runs.

So now let's break it down further and find another group of people that specialize in breaking stuff, and we'll have them test the code. They write test cases, break it, find edge cases; all of these are different tasks. Now most of the individuals that complete the tasks don't do anything else but that task. The copilot stands over all of them and acts as the air traffic control and makes sure all the pieces get done and all the pieces fit back together correctly.

That would be how we would build an iPad app. Break it down into tasks, assign, delegate, and manage.

I want to give you a specific example that was being run for *JAMA Oncology*, and it was a collaboration with Harvard Business School. What they wanted to do was take a bunch of CAT scans of cancer patients and train an algorithm to act like an oncologist and detect cancer.

The way that lung cancer is primarily detected today is

you have experts in hospitals. You get sent out to pathology, they send it out to experts, and those experts review it, look at it, and then make an assessment based on the CAT scan, based on the data they have.

There's a very small number of these experts that do the majority of lung cancer cases in the United States. And they're a small pool of people that look at these things, analyze them, and make their expert opinions. We wanted to see if it was possible to create an algorithm that could do it as good as or better than that small group of experts.

So we got all the data, we partnered with the research organization, we worked with Harvard Business School and a bunch of PhDs to set up a very structured experiment. We broke it into its pieces: different types of algorithms that need to be used, see it, find it, detect it, it's all these different tasks.

Then we came across a problem: false positives.

Humans can detect false positives, but computers had a harder time distinguishing. So we broke it down into all these smaller, really complex mathematical and algorithmic problems; we taskified that, and we launched those independently to our community. Then we had our people compete on it.

The end result is we now have a paper that is just being published in *JAMA Oncology*, and we have an algorithm that is as accurate as this panel of experts at detecting lung cancer in CAT scans.

This can be available to everybody at the time of a CAT scan. This can be available to everybody across the globe, not just the people that have access to this panel of fifty experts. And not only are we going to be as accurate as this panel, our algorithm will continue to get smarter, it will be more accurate than even the best possible oncologists as it gets more and more data. The freelancers that solved this problem aren't people that are experts in cancer, they're people that are experts in math.

We were able to break this problem down to find those experts, to find those people that had these crazy math skills, and they could apply them to this problem.

Paul: What was your main takeaway from this experience?

Mike: You can't stay stuck in your old mindset. We have a tendency to get comfortable and stay put. We wait for something to break before we fix it. The Gig Mindset shakes all that up.

We had a big goal and a strict timeline. If we hadn't

broken things down, really took taskification to heart, I don't think we would have been successful.

STEVE RADER

Paul: Can you talk about how NASA has engaged freelancers, and how some of your contests use Taskfication?

Steve: The use of freelancers and the Gig Economy is an area where Paul is way ahead of us at NASA. Our starting point with crowds was to use prizes and challenges to solve problems—taking a specific problem, narrowing it down, and then putting a bounty out there to find the right person in the crowd to solve the problem.

There are some really amazing stories about how the crowd has provided just the right hard-to-find skill or expertise; I'll share this one. NASA was trying to do solar flare prediction with a two-hour prediction capability, which is just not enough time. Instead, the agency wanted to double that to four hours to maximize safety for crew members doing space walks.

On the surface of the Earth, we are normally protected from solar radiation by its magnetic field. Most of the time, the most damage a solar flare will cause for us on the ground would be temporary issues like cell phone outages. However, for people in space like astronauts out working on a space walk, a solar flare can be much more dangerous. Without the protection of special shielding, a solar flare can damage their cells and give them cancer or it can affect electronics controlling their space suits.

NASA has a set of models that can predict flares two hours before they happen, kind of like weather prediction models, but we really needed that capability to extend beyond two hours. When you're out on a space walk, it takes a good amount of time to stow your tools, to get all the way back into the space station, to repressurize the airlock, to get out of your space suit, and then to get into a part of the space station with extra radiation shielding. An alert to the crew only two hours before a solar flare is cutting it close.

So, our group worked with the heliophysics group—studying the nature and physics of the sun and how it affects the solar system—to post a crowdsourced challenge on Innocentive and asked, "How can we increase solar prediction time?" People from all over the world with all sorts of backgrounds worked on the problem. The guy who won the challenge was a retired cell phone engineer who also happened to have an undergraduate degree in heliophysics. During his career, he worked with the math used to extract signals from noise that allows us to have those higher and higher data rates on our cell phones. It was that realization that he could apply the mathematics

from the cell phone industry into this heliophysics problem that led him to create an algorithm that could predict
solar flares up to eight hours out—a 4X increase in performance. The whole process really got our science team to
look at a whole new way to attack problems and predic-
tions. That's just one way a diverse set of skills that you
find in these large online communities can provide value.

Solutions are technology stacks applied to a problem,
a collection of different technologies put together in a
very specific way to get that novel solution that leads
to higher performance. What's going on right now in
the world is there is just this explosion of technology,
with building blocks like blockchain, 3D printing, open
APIs, drones, and low-cost sensors. All these things
work across lots of domains and they're multiplying
the possibilities of solutions that can be applied to various problems.

What that means for us at NASA is the increasing possibility to reach 2X, 3X, 5X, 10X performance improvement
in solutions to some of our problems. That's a massive
undertaking, but crowdsourcing is a way to tap into that
explosion of technological possibility. Finding all those
skills and the people that have knowledge of these other
domains is a huge asset. With complex problems, these
crowdsourcing platforms are proving to be effective
tools in finding people with the unique skills and exper-

tise mix to find unique solutions that pull from diverse business sectors.

We realized in working with lots of different crowdsourcing communities on lots of different types of products that crowds have an incredible capacity—with the right mechanisms in place—to match that capacity with a specific need. We are seeing that this is not limited to crowdsourced prizes and challenges, but is a common characteristic across the freelance and gig work communities and platforms as well. This is what has attracted us to what Paul is doing with taskification and the future of work. As fast as things are changing, it is becoming clear that we need to pivot to start leveraging this new model if we hope to keep up and stay relevant.

DYAN FINKHOUSEN

Paul: Dyan, we've heard from a few people about how taskification can be used to create open contests for freelancers. How do you look at it from a heavy industrial point of view?

Dyan: Taskification is an essential component of our process. In a heavy industrial organization—we solve for highly complex and technical opportunities—and for safety, compliance, speed, and efficiency. To insert freelance resource methodology into that heavy industrial process, we had to develop a playbook that not only wouldn't compromise performance, but would enhance outcomes for the teams.

Taskification enables us to disaggregate a complex problem into a set of more granular components. The Gig Economy enables us to access a virtually limitless bench of highly specialized resources. With our complex problem taskified into a more precise set of granular components—we now have greater freedom to match each problem component to expertise that we source from our own team or from expert markets in the Gig Economy.

Precision resourcing with greater reach has been invaluable for performance, and the trick has been to do so in a compliant, scalable and cost-effective manner—to increase rather than diminish agility. This would not have been possible without early and sustained partnership with intellectual property counsel, finance, and sourcing.

I'll share a great example that illustrates how we take heavy industrial priorities through our expert operating system process, and specifically how taskification plays a role in that process.

One of our early programs was designed to support our oil and gas business unit and their client, who were collectively responding to marketplace feedback regarding the climate and community impact of onshore operations.

On the face of it—climate and community impact of onshore operations—a broad scope with the potential for many solutions that could improve the outcome for all. To drive the best possible result, we coached the team to narrow the scope so we could focus on a solution set to address the greatest drivers of the climate and community impact. That enabled us to taskify the solution paths, and expand the expert community with whom we could collaborate on the solution paths.

Our taskification process yielded a focus scope that the team believed could generate great outcomes: reducing the volume of materials transportation to and from onshore operation sites. Transportation of materials to and from these sites meant that large trucks were carrying heavy loads through communities located adjacent to the operation sites—contributing to additional traffic congestion, emissions, wear on the roads, etc. The team believed that by taskifying, we would identify innovations that could reduce the need for heavy materials in onshore operations. If we could reduce the transport requirements, we would improve the climate and community impact of onshore operations.

And the team was right. We designed a set of innovation

scopes that focused on reducing the amount of water and proppant needed for onshore operations, and we reached out to a global community of experts using an open innovation approach. The community responded with a strong portfolio of over 250 innovation options, enabling our team to activate collaborations with multiple expert organizations and build a portfolio of solution paths.

By taking a more precise approach to solution path development through taskification, and by collaborating with a more expansive community of experts through open innovation, the team was able to improve innovation performance by more than 10x.

Paul: Do you think you could have been as successful without taskifying that project?

Dyan: I think we would have found a solution. Eventually. But it would have likely taken a lot longer, cost more, and had less of an overall impact.

TUCKER MAX

Paul: Tucker, Scribe Media breaks down the publishing process into digestible chunks. Can you talk more about how that process came to be?

Tucker: Taskification was pretty easy.

First, I had to find the problem. There are people out there with books in their heads, but no time to write. I was talking to a friend, listening to her frustrations over time management and what she wanted to say in a book and what it would do to her life, and it hit me. I told her I could do that.

She asked me how much it would cost.

I was literally like, "I don't know, 10 grand," because I didn't really need the money. I was like, "Ten grand is enough to make it worth my while and fun," but I looked at it legitimately as just a fun project and that's it.

I immediately went to the whiteboard—yes, I have a whiteboard in my house—and I wrote out every single step in writing a book. It took me a while, because the first time I wrote it, I'm like, "There's like ten steps. Right? Just ten steps."

Then I started actually thinking about it.

I'm like, "Hold on a minute. Each step has another ten or twenty steps embedded in it." It went from ten steps to seventy steps to where it is now. The process seemed so freaking complex. It's not actually. It got overcomplicated, and now we've dialed it back a little bit.

For example, before you even start writing a book, there's

positioning. Positioning is the most important thing you do with your book by far. Positioning is understanding what place your book occupies in the mind of the reader. To get that seems like kind of easy. It's not.

There are three basic steps you have to do to position your book. Paul went through these.

The first set of questions are our objectives: Why are you writing this book? What do you want your audience to get, and what do you want to get? We have to be very clear with the author on that, and we have to make sure their objectives actually are realistic and achievable.

Once we get objectives, then we go to audience. Who is your primary audience? Who's your secondary audience? Tell me who they are. We need to know who they are and why they're going to care about this book. To do that, what we do is we go really deep. We create an avatar. Tell me about the pain they have because they haven't read the book. What transformation are they going to go through if they read your book and they apply it? What's the benefit they're going to get? You've got to really, deeply understand that.

The next step is idea. Everyone wants to start with idea, but that's wrong, because your idea is just some crap in your head. An objective needs to be anchored in reality.

You look at your idea, and now you have to adjust the three things and make sure they all flow, which is what we call the North Star statement.

You put them all together and it says, "I want to write a book to blank, to get blank," whatever your objectives are, "And I'll do this by teaching blank," which is your audience, "About blank," which is your subject, "And to do that, I'll reach my ultimate goal of whatever blank," right?

Then you brainstorm the chapters, right? Then you structure them, make sure that you've got the right chapters in the right order. Then you outline the book. Then once the outline is done, you interview.

You do your content interviews. Those are recorded. Then you get those transcribed. Then you take those transcriptions and you translate them into book prose. Then you polish the prose into something enjoyable. Entertaining. Then you revise with the author, you do edits, revisions.

Then, guess what? You've got a freaking book. I mean, there are a few more high-level steps—getting a cover, marketing, community development—but those are the basic steps to writing a book.

You've got to think of this like Russian nesting dolls.

Writing, publishing, marketing. Then within writing, there's six nested tasks. With publishing, there's like eight or ten. Within distribution or within marketing, there's an infinite number in marketing honestly, depending on what level down you want to go to.

Taskification. It's looking at your big goal—publish a book—and cracking open that nesting doll. Find the smaller tasks. Break those down even further. Once you've got the smallest doll in your hand, now you're ready to start.

BREAK DOWN TO BUILD UP

Henry Ford turned eighty-four steps into an unstoppable industry. He revolutionized the assembly line, factories, and industry as we know it. He did this by changing his mindset, approaching his problem in a new way, and resetting his default. There is nothing that Ford did that you can't do.

Breaking down your tasks takes time. You have to know what the end result will be before you understand the path to get there. Now that you've seen how this process can work for industry leaders, maybe it doesn't seem so outrageous. Maybe you're starting to believe what I've been saying these last few chapters.

Now it's time to put your mind to the task. I've been giving you homework this entire book, but now we're going to really stretch those muscles. I want you to see firsthand that this works. Don't skip the next step. Follow these Go-Do tasks and you'll see just what the Gig Mindset can do for you.

This is the first step to understand the power of the T.I.D.E Model and will ensure that you are set up for success moving forward. As we discussed in the chapter, getting to work in the morning and creating an impactful slide deck are all made up of tasks. Now that you are thinking about working with freelance experts around the world, let's get started with a project that you want to tackle.

1. Define a successful outcome. Start at the end and imagine the finished project. The first thing I recommend is taking some time and really understanding your goal or vision. Write this down in a simple paragraph.

2. Who are the stakeholders; who is the primary audience for this work?

3. What are all the individual deliverables for the project? These are components that have specific timelines and scope and could be assigned to a person on the team or a freelancer. Take some time to brainstorm at this phase, as it has always been helpful for me to put more down at this stage and refine later.

4. Are there items that can be combined/streamlined? Now take some time to understand each project and write down what needs to be done/delivered (scope, description).

5. How important is each component? Assign priorities: high/medium/low.

6. What is a realistic initial timeline for the project? Take a look at the tasks and get a good understanding of any dependencies for the work (e.g., the wireframes for a website would need to be completed before the development would get started). Write all of this into a simple initial draft for the project. I often share this with freelancers as I get started to get their feedback. It also helps set expectations.

7. Remember, you are now working with a network of experts. Ask for their thoughts and best practices as you go along.

IDENTIFY

"Focus on being productive instead of busy."

—TIM FERRISS, *THE 4-HOUR WORKWEEK: ESCAPE 9-5, LIVE ANYWHERE, AND JOIN THE NEW RICH*

If there is one universal constant in business, it's the concept of "death by slideshow."

Either you've sat in a meeting bored to tears by a bad slideshow, or you've wasted hours of your life putting one together. It's not the program's fault. We are responsible for the bad reputation the software has gained. We clog the screen with confusing graphics, overload the slides with text, and read verbatim for forty slides instead of presenting an idea.

At any point in my career, I can remember sitting down at my computer to design yet another presentation. I'd arrange the text, find some key art, and cycle through the canned list of transitions. I was very process focused instead of outcome focused.

Imagine a room full of vice presidents and someone who needs to get their idea across. They have prepared, the entire team is there, and then comes the presentation: sixty-plus slides of ten-point font and bad clip art. You can probably guess how well that went.

I started to realize that I wasn't learning how to deliver a better presentation. I was learning the features of the presentation software. I was training myself to be in a job several rungs below where I was. It was crazy.

As chief of staff, I did dozens of presentations, and I must have seen hundreds more. What I found more effective was to start at the end, at the outcome. Once I knew the outcome, I worked backward to build the right story. Since I knew the points I had to make, I could focus my research around key areas. I had emotional beats built in. By focusing on my goal, everything else fell into place.

We just broke down taskification. If I know that my goal is "convince others to see my perspective," I can figure out the path. It involves a presentation for a meeting. That presentation is going to need research, videos, motion graphics, and custom data visualizations (areas where specific experts can be invaluable). All of that has to fit into a narrative that is engaging and informative. Finally, I need to present it all in an impressive way so that I don't lose my audience's attention.

This means I need to have data to present, but I also have to show it off in specific ways. Different charts can convey different meanings. Colors have emotional effects on people. This is a lot to keep in mind when designing a presentation, and it's impossible to become an expert in every single step. Professional designers study these things, and they understand how they impact and influence an audience.

Before I reset my defaults, I would do everything myself. I would stay up late researching topics, often jumping from one website to the next until I found myself lost down the rabbit hole. I taught myself the software—at least I thought I did, after twenty years and hundreds of slide decks—and I'd throw together a passable presentation. Finally, I'd spice it up with some jokes and storytelling. As you may have guessed, holding a book with my name on it, I'm a bit of a storyteller. I can find the narrative. But that's just one skill, and I was expecting myself to master many.

It wasn't until I started working with a network of experts and really studying the space that I learned about the importance of structured storytelling and the power of design. If I was going to try and push an idea forward, I wanted to put the best pitch out there.

Getting a presentation ready for an executive review was a massive undertaking, but the people involved were only thinking about the process and not the result. It was like designing a house based only on the building blocks. It needed walls, a roof, a floor, a toilet, and a kitchen, but you never considered what made it feel like a home. All of these presentations arrived in shambles, created by a committee that wasn't outcome focused. Then the executives said, "I don't have an hour to spare; can you just hurry through this?"

After engaging in the Gig Mindset, I saw the various tasks that I needed to spread out. Using a number of websites, I found freelancers with exactly the skills I needed to build the presentation. There were researchers who specialized in my topic, designers with portfolios of brilliant presentations, and speechwriters able to take my notes and turn them into a cohesive argument.

That's the key to identification. You're more than capable of designing your own presentation, but is that the best use of your time? If you engaged with freelancers, your vision wouldn't change. Imagine yourself in a new role as a Hollywood film director. You're assembling a team of creative and technical experts, but they are all focused on delivering *your* idea and *your* goal.

A great example is market research, a staple of any business. It used to be if I wanted to find out market research, I would go and get a big firm, sit down, and write a SOW—statement of work—and spend months and months on a project. Then the firm would throw a partner-level resource, build a team of people right out of college, and the snowball would just keep growing. They'd book a bunch of revenue, and we do a market sizing or strategy project.

Now, I'm literally reaching out to market experts that are consultants, and I can do two or three projects simultaneously. My current market researcher has a PhD and lives in India. Not only is he incredibly talented and knowledgeable, but his worldview and experience are far different from my own.

I was working on a project and needed some detailed information. I posted the work order on a Saturday morning, and within two hours he raised his hand and took the job. I was blown away by the quality of his research and the depth of his insight and recommendations. He sees problems from different angles, which leads to diversity of thought.

That's worth calling out. Diversity of thought, the kind you'll get with a network of trusted experts, helps you and your ideas stand out. It helps your presentation feel unique.

I get the diversity of thought. And each time I reach out, I will learn a little bit more. For the same price that I would have done one large project with a big firm, I can do a bunch of smaller market research and strategy projects and piece them together since I have the vision of the outcome.

The diversity is incredibly powerful. Each person brings in their own point of view, a wider field of value to the project. I'll bet a lot of you reading this book have struggled with the idea of hiring a large consulting firm. "It'd be really great if I could hire this group, or if I had the budget for that company." I'm here to tell you that there is a better way. It's not just about saving money; it's about using your budget for the highest possible impact.

It is easy to get obsessed with the tasks, with the minutiae, and forget the outcome. To live the Gig Mindset, you need to be outcome oriented. When you first taskify, and you break your goal down into smaller chunks, it can be overwhelming. "It's eighty-four steps to build this Model T? I'll never get it done!"

What you've done is identify the work, and you've realized it is more than you could ever do alone. Well, no one said this was supposed to be just you. Remember, it's about the outcome. When I was chief of staff, I had an incredible team working alongside me. Our presentations had plenty of heart, but they weren't focused on the results, just the journey. That made them less effective than they could have been.

So the first and most important step is to identify the work that can be done by you, your team, or your network of freelancers. If it's difficult, don't feel bad. This is where a lot of people struggle. It is about the willingness to give up control, to exercise a little trust.

"But I'm the only person that can do this. It would take more time to explain this to somebody than just doing it myself. Oh, I had a bad experience with a freelancer once."

These are the excuses we give ourselves. There are endless reasons not to do something, or to hold onto the old ways, but you have to shake yourself loose. You have to reset your defaults. Most importantly, you have to recognize your greatest limitation: time.

I remember a conversation I had with one of my designers. He was concerned about getting certain details just right, to the point that he said he was the *only person* that could do the project. I asked him, "There are 7 billion people on the planet, and you're the *only* one who can do this?" It was a shock. When he took time to think about it, he realized he'd fallen into a fixed mindset. Where was his radical curiosity? Why did he have to do everything himself?

Do CEOs have more time than everyone else? No. They have different support structures. They compartmentalize processes so the employees can run without their direct supervision. They trust their staff to execute a vision, and they define that vision as clearly as possible so it can be understood down to the lowest-level employee. The idea that you can personally take on every project for your business is just not possible. What could your time be better spent doing?

If you have great ideas and visions for the future, don't bog yourself down with small tasks. Identify what can be spread out. Identify your new team. Get to work.

MIKE MORRIS

Paul: Mike, how do you use identification at Topcoder? How do you decide what to do, delay, drop, or delegate?

Mike: That's about having a trusted network. It's about knowing your freelancers and what they can do.

Paul: How do you make that decision?

Mike: Employees come with different skillsets, strengths, and weaknesses. Everyone is different.

At Topcoder, we have statistics on every one of our people. Think of it like a sport. Baseball has statistics on batters, pitchers, base runners, fielders, and the bullpen. They look at them independently because you very rarely have somebody that's a great hitter, an awesome bullpen, and a great fielder. You very rarely have people that are across more than one of those disciplines, and we found the same to be true in Topcoder.

In my history I think it was only one person I can remember that was red rated—red means the top winner—in two different disciplines.

There was this legend that one person was red for a day in three disciplines, and we have no proof of that because it was not true. That's the Loch Ness monster of coding. But my point is that people are really good at certain things, and we looked at it and said, "We want to give people the opportunity to show off their best skills."

Our algorithms and data science are under one discipline. Our software development is a second discipline. And our creative designer is the third discipline. And inside those disciplines then you can segment it by type of algorithmic problem, or technology, or type of design even further, but it's all for the purpose of giving that person the opportunity that shows off their skillsets.

There's no one person capable of doing everything you want at the level you aim to hit. That goes for you too. You can't do everything yourself. Once you realize that, once you recognize your limits, it's easy to find the people that can take on that effort.

Paul: So when you have the right people...

Mike: Then you can decide what to do. That's how you identify the tasks to delegate out.

STEVE RADER

Paul: NASA is filled with some of the smartest, most innovative people on the planet. How do you identify when to collaborate with freelancers?

Steve: We as a society have conflated the ideas of innovation and innovative people—that those are one and the same. People that have the innovative ideas are also the people that need to implement them. But that's not true; if you are looking for an innovative solution to your problem, you really need these other experts and viewpoints to find the ideas and technologies you will need for that innovative solution.

This all boils down to utilizing outside perspectives to find your solution, and then bringing those perspectives inside. You may also need to go find some expertise that you don't have, but in both cases, you don't necessarily have to go hire all of that. You can actually engage crowds to find what you need.

We did a galactic cosmic ray challenge a while back where we asked: how do you protect humans from galactic cosmic rays?

The seven finalists were all nuclear physicists from universities around the world who had put in forty to eighty hours each toward a solution, trying to collaborate to find this answer—all for a chance at a $20,000 prize. That's amazing access to a community that's really hard to mobilize any other way. If you ask, "How would you go hire nuclear physicists to go work on your problem?" Just the logistics of it is hard.

In fact, if the challenge can be used by the participants to develop new skills or technologies that they can use in the future, they recognize that whether they win the prize or not, they're getting something out of the process. When NASA does its Centennial Challenges, which are similar to the X Prize-brand challenges, they put a million dollars out there and say, "Okay, who's going to be the first one? Who can solve this impossible problem?"

What they find are companies, individuals, and academia that come together to form teams, collaborate, and build. In fact, the amount of research and development funds that are invested in these efforts ends up being four times the value of the prize. That is a 4X multiplier on research and development dollars you just got out of a challenge. In exchange, the competitors are given the chance to work in the field, get recognition, and build up their skills. That's what attracts these incredibly capable and creative people toward freelance opportunities.

In the case of the DARPA self-driving car challenge, if you go look at the people who now have companies around self-driving cars, they were all competitors in that competition. Not the winners necessarily, but the competitors. These competitions provide the framework and a target where they're building the technologies and working out all of the kinks. That's different and more collaborative than traditional technology development efforts. That's what attracts these incredibly capable and creative people toward freelance opportunities. This is a chance to work in the field, get recognition, and build skills.

It's just a really fascinating model. It's all intersecting; it's all the same tool—the capacity of people outside of their normal jobs to contribute in real and significant ways, whether that's freelance, gig, or contest. Those are all variants of matching what someone has to offer with someone who has a need.

I like to describe it as matching a need with somebody who can meet that need. Airbnb is matching rooms with people that need a place to stay. Uber is matching people that need rides with people that have cars and can drive. Contests turn out to be a really effective way to match ideas and expertise to solve a hard problem when maybe it isn't clear who might be able to do it.

The scenario usually goes like this: I've had ten scientists working on this problem for years and they haven't come up with a solution, so I'm going to put a challenge out there. I don't know who's going to come. Sure enough, someone in the crowd comes up with an innovative solution, almost every time—many times from someone outside of the domain of the problem. In fact, there's data from a study by Harvard Business School that shows that 70 percent of the time successful solutions came from solvers that were not in the same domain as the problem owner.[25]

Well, that's a game-changer for R&D. For years we've

25   Kevin J. Boudreau, Karim R. Lakhani, and Michael Neietti, "Performance Responses to Competition across Skill-Levels in Rank Order Tournaments: Field Evidence and Implications for Tournament Design," *Harvard Business School*, January 8, 2016, https://dash.harvard.edu/bitstream/handle/1/11508222/boudreau%2clakhani%2cmenietti_performance-response-to-competition-across-skill-levels.pdf?sequence=3.

been taking a team of chemists, putting them in a chemistry lab, and saying, "Go find the latest and greatest chemistry innovation." Now, we open it up to the crowd and because crowds are super diverse, they can find and put together the technologies in a way that those chemists would have never thought about. The crowd can come up with that innovative solution. It's amazing. It is amazing how often it works. It is amazing *how* it works.

It turns out there are some super-solver people out there that are just passionate about problem-solving. We had one guy who won our Mars Bounds challenge. He went on to win seventeen other challenges on the Innocentive platform. He happened to be one of these multi-domain kind of super nerds that knew all of the math for everything and could do some amazing work. That's a really interesting resource to tap into because, in an organization, that person would probably be wedged into a set of tasks that was very narrow and wasn't taking full advantage of his capacity. In this kind of Wild West of problems, where there's challenges coming from every industry through the platform, he was basically exercising what his muscles were best at, what his brain was best at doing.

People actually want to learn new things. If you don't have a project that is challenging you to grow in your skills, then how do you learn?

There was a $1,500,000 contest to help Homeland Security run on Kaggle (a community of 1.6 million data scientists specializing in machine learning) to get a better algorithm for detecting weapons on people as they go through the airport scanners. We had a freshman at Berkeley who won $100,000 who had decided to work on the challenge just so he could become more proficient in machine learning. He said he wanted to learn machine learning and this looked like a cool project he could use to apply the techniques in the textbook.

He literally went online to figure out machine learning. He was a software guy, so he had the background to access and use the machine learning APIs/software, but he wasn't a mathematician or traditional data scientist. He sets up a machine learning solution just like the online training says and then he reads the part that says that the machine learning is going to work better if you provide it more training data. Homeland Security had provided participants with thousands of images to help build their algorithms. But in machine learning, you really need more like tens and hundreds of thousands.

Our guy from Berkley just so happened to also have experience with video games and knew that with a 3D graphics rendering tool called Blender, you can write scripts to generate lifelike people with a variety of skin textures, skeleton dimensions, and body mass. He basically wrote a script to generate thousands of different people with weapons in different positions on their body in a way that looked very similar to the scanner images that DHS provided. Then he took that data set and ran that through his machine learning model. His solution ended up performing in the top ten. Homeland Security literally asked him if he was interested in a job during the presentation of his design. They admitted that they would have never have thought to do that. In fact, they might have saved a lot of time and money in generating their data setup if they'd understood that technique.

It's that kind of innovation that you don't get from people inside the box.

Paul: So it came down to the people?

Steve: Knowing the tasks, breaking them down, it got us thinking. It helped us ask the right questions, find the right people. That's when you can identify the work to do and drop. You have to find the right people first.

DYAN FINKHOUSEN

Paul: Now Dyan, you're looking at this a little differently at GE. When you're deciding the four Ds—Do, Drop, Delegate—how do you find the right talent?

Dyan: Finding the right talent is the real magic of the Gig Economy. There are so many expert marketplaces available today that we have more freedom than ever to recruit a great talent match.

Historically we've generally relied on our full-time employees and supplier organizations resources for our operations. If we just reframe the way we approach resource design and use tasks and competencies rather than jobs as our base units of work, and then assume we can augment our resource pool of full-time employees and suppliers with access to a virtually limitless bench of experts through the Gig Economy—we have much greater freedom and precision in the way we resource our operations.

This approach opens up a new world of opportunity for our teams—they can be so much more successful by taking this precision approach to resourcing operations.

To illustrate the point, we'll jump back to my example with the onshore operations program.

When we focused on generating innovative solutions that would reduce the need for water and proppant in onshore operations—we were able to identify a corresponding set of competencies that we believed would be required to generate the target innovations. By taskifying the target expertise into more granular competencies—this again provided us greater freedom to not only look for experts and solution paths in the onshore operations industry, but also to reach into other industry sectors for experts and solutions that might be a good fit...to reach beyond "the usual suspects" and connect with experts that might not be known to us, but who could help us drive a better outcome.

With the taxonomy of target competencies in hand, we applied open innovation methodology to connect with a community of around two million technical and scientific experts to seek their help with the scope. The competency taxonomy enabled us to directly connect with experts whose profile matched any of our target competencies. Our use of open innovation methodology enabled us to extend our reach to experts who could also be highly valuable collaborators due to their interest, ideas, and additional relevant competencies.

As a quick summary—we addressed identification with the taskification of the scope, a detailed competency taxonomy, and expert community mapping that leverages core and cross-pollination talent pools.

So the ability to taskify the problem statement allows us to reach into industries where we can find solutions and experts who may have very relevant applications to the problem in the host industry. So we can reach across industries with taskification, we can reach across industries and pull in highly disruptive solutions because we can break the problem components down and pull in solution components that may be relevant in a new context.

When you read the examples from Mike or Steve or Tucker or John, you can see what I mean. I've got twenty employees in a box trying to engineer a way out, but an astrophysicist came up with the solution by looking at an entirely different problem. That cross talk, that diversification of thought, drives innovation and solutions.

Identification is tied to taskification in this way. When we know exactly what we need to do, we can easily decide what we need to delegate, delay, and drop. The taskification of the work allows us to pull in not only the traditional experts, but also allows us to reach across industries and pull in brilliant solutions, brilliant expertise in a way that might not have been possible if you didn't taskify the work. That's why the steps in the T.I.D.E. Model are important.

This is a very, very big change for heavy industry. It used to be that you would taskify your work, but then you'd do it all internally. It had to be done inside. There was no way to delay a task or delegate. There were walls, boundaries that kept you from reaching out and scaling.

If you taskify work and look across the boundaries of where you're sourcing experts, if you just assume there are no boundaries to where you can find the best expert or the best solution, you can source better work, better outcomes in a much more efficient manner.

That is the guiding principle that we use in order to source expertise, source solutions. It's a taskification of work, and the assumption that there are *no boundaries* to where you can find the best solutions, the best experts, the right expert. It's again looking at the world assuming that you can conduct business without boundaries, and I say that to be intentionally provocative. We all understand there are boundaries, but they're just newly defined.

Imagine what you could get done if there were no limits on who you could consult, who you could bring in from a network.

Another quick example, and this gets I think to Paul's other point, is one where we're using internal experts. So it's not external freelance resources, but it's basically the taskification and it's the sourcing of expert support across the boundaries of our own business within the context of our own business.

Confused yet? Let me break this down.

So one of our teams was a startup. A couple of years back, they were starting up a new business within our company. They were asked to deliver a pretty big goal, so they had a small team and this was our additive manufacturing team—to define that quickly, additive manufacturing is the process of joining materials to make objects from 3D model data, usually layer upon layer, as opposed to subtractive manufacturing methodologies.

They were being incubated within our aviation business unit and had been asked to work across the boundaries of our industrial business units to connect with all the engineers, the technologists, and the product managers across the company to talk about what was possible with additive manufacturing, and how we might be able to increase the productivity of our manufacturing operations by deploying additive capabilities.

Again, small team, and additive, and a big goal. They were asked to deliver $5 billion in productivity across the industrial businesses operations in the matter of a few years. So we collaborated with the additive team and broke down their problem statement. At the end of the day, the team needed to deliver $5 billion in productivity gains for all of the industrial business units.

We know that they needed to meet with all of the teams, educate all of the industrial engineering and product teams across the company around the world, and they needed to do so with limited resources. And then they needed to collaborate on road maps that considered the deployment of additive. So we basically provided them with a platform, a website that was configured to support digital collaboration.

Documentation is *critical* if you are going to bring in experts. We were able to create a digital record of the education materials and the ideas for how additive could have benefited different product groups, and begin to collect information about the potential impact of converting traditional manufactured products into additive manufacturer products.

Then the digital team was able to prioritize the opportunities using the digital platform. The digital platform basically allowed a digital record of the various tasks to progress through the product management tool-gating system.

The results? The team was able to use a task-based approach and a collaborative approach, and they were able to achieve that $5 billion goal in a matter of nine months. It was just breaking down the work, applying a broader expert ecosystem to that work, because the work was taskified. It was broken down into various components, and then it was made accessible through a digital platform.

It immediately expanded the reach and the pace of the team so that they could accomplish their goal in a much, much more effective way.

Paul: For you, the expansion opened up what work was possible.

Dyan: Before, we wouldn't have been able to do as much internal work. A lot of the tasks would get dropped. By finding the right experts for our tasks and breaking down the borders to engage with new teams, we were able to delegate so much more.

TUCKER MAX

Paul: Tucker, how did you identify the work your company needed to do in order to be competitive in the publishing industry?

Tucker: For Scribe it was easy, because I already owned a publishing company, right? I had already done this with my own books, so I knew how to do it and I knew the people that I would work with, so it was easy for me. The problem for us came not for the first couple ones. It came once we started scaling.

When you've got ten books, that's plenty of work for you and your friends and that's all you need. But when you have one hundred books, that's more work than you and your friends can handle.

We had to come up with an entire process because, again we're not doing a book. We're doing books at scale. We had to come up with a process for finding, testing, vetting, and onboarding freelancers, which is a very big process.

I would actually add in another step. This is a really good example of where I've got embedded knowledge, tacit knowledge that I'm not making explicit. There's actually a step prior. Before you go find people, you need to know what you're looking for.

You've got to identify exactly what you need. I think that's step one. That was my embedded knowledge, because I know what a book designer looks like. I know what they need to be able to do. I know what a writer needs to be able to do. I already know that. But if someone were managing this process on their own, that's actually the step where everyone would get messed up, because the next step's easy.

It's about a vision, a concept that everyone involved makes happen.

Finding people, there's so many marketplaces for writers. There's Readz, there's Mediabistro, there's Scribe. Honestly, there are ten sites already. You can go on Craigslist in big cities and find them. Like right now in New York.

No, seriously. Now. In New York, you can find all our writers on Craigslist. Finding people is not the problem. That used to be the problem, but in 2019 there are marketplaces everywhere. The problem is not finding people. The problem is understanding what you need, identifying *what* and *who*. For most people, that's a really big problem. What exactly do you need?

Especially for complicated processes. In a simple process, it's not an issue. Like, you know what you need in a house painter. You need someone who can paint the freaking house. You don't necessarily know what you need in a writer or an editor. You could need developmental editing, evaluation editing, content editing, line editing, copy editing, or proofreading. They're all very different, and they mean different things. If you don't know what they mean to an expert, you're going to do it wrong. You've got to get very clear on what service or skill you need.

For almost any of these tasks, there's going to be at least a couple marketplaces. You want to find that marketplace, then figure out a way to test their skills, because here's the thing: I am a great writer, and I don't trust myself to look at a writer's resumé or CV and just know their ability based on that.

When we're hiring scribes, we do have a place where we want them to put in the books they have written, the articles, the blogs, et cetera. It's not that it doesn't matter. That's just kind of the entry fee to get in. If you've never written a book before, then we're not going to bother. Multiple books actually. Three is our minimum for us to consider you. But once you've written three books, you have met the minimum bar for becoming a Scribe.

We've had Pulitzer Prize-winning writers and Emmy winning writers who did not make the cut, and it wasn't because they can't write. It's because their specific skills were not a good fit for our process, because our process is not just who's the best writer. I mean if our scribes couldn't get on the phone with you, and create rapport with you, and understand you, then being a good writer just isn't enough.

We have a lot of our scribes who are still growing as writers. They're not someone I would hire to just write something, at least not yet. But what they're great at is creating rapport with authors, and understanding authors, and building relationships with authors, and getting the author's voice and intention onto the page in an authentic way.

You can do that and you just have to be a solid to good writer. All of our scribes are like that. Some just have an edge in making words effortlessly entertaining. We wouldn't find out any of this if we didn't vet them.

It needs to be a multistage process, and you need to look at every interaction with them as a test. We do. Our process has been a little haphazard in the past, but now it's very dialed in for hiring scribes.

It begins when you fill out the form. After you fill it out, you get an email back from us. It's kind of a pain honestly, and it's a pain for the scribe on purpose. Because if you aren't willing to go through that process, and do those details, and put in that work, then you're not going to fit in our process well. We try and make the evaluation process at least as hard, and difficult, and demanding as the actual work they're going to do, at least if not more so.

We look at every single interaction as a test, as a part of that test. When you turn in your editing sample, it's not just the editing. It's how quickly did you do it. We give you a forty-eight-hour turnaround. Did you turn it around in five hours, or did you turn it around five minutes before it was due? That absolutely matters. We look at that a lot.

If you're late, if you miss anything anywhere in the process, you're done. You're out. Because it's sort of like if someone can't even make an effort on a first date, what are they going to be like in a relationship? It's the exact same thing. You should be under the assumption that everyone is trying to get the gig, so you need to actually pay very close attention. Any negative signal in the courtship phase, if you want to call it that, is a red flag.

You have to define your process, figure out exactly what you need from these people. As you say, you need to identify what you need to do and delegate. If you're uncertain, you're going in blind.

JOHN WINSOR

Paul: What do you think is the key takeaway for identification?

John: The decisions you make here—what to do, delay, drop, or delegate—shape the scope of the project and help you communicate your expectations to your network.

One person, one employee, can't do everything. That's just not possible. So what happens? You delay the project, or you drop it completely. That's why you need to build that trusted network. Now, instead of pushing a task aside, you can delegate it to an expert and do another task yourself.

Companies are discovering that, by stepping out of the

normal boundaries and engaging with the freelance market, they can find the experts they need to accomplish any task.

When NASA has a very difficult problem in the field of heliophysics—the study of the sun's effect on the solar system—and their top ten scientists haven't made progress in a decade, they don't cross their arms and wait for a solution.

Where they're seeing a lot of success is from posting the questions on platforms and in contests. The people that win those have these exponential gains and knowledge, or know people with that knowledge.

Remember, it's the retired cell phone engineer that studied heliophysics in college and actually learned about radiation in his cell phone work. That diversity of thought leads to innovation and invention you just can't get with a fixed mindset. The heliophysicists inside NASA don't have that experience.

In my mind, it's making internal team members superhuman. How do we create Iron Man suits with the technology and the knowledge of this democratized knowledge work basis? With this expert intelligence, how do we make internal teams and internal team members superhuman, super powerful?

My sense is our world is so full of abundance that to solve problems in an efficient way, no one human can do it. It's really about our network, building our networks. Our network teams. I'm really fascinated lately by freelancers that are almost superhuman, and they're micro-entrepreneurs.

When you realize you have this wealth of talent just waiting to be engaged, it changes what you can do. Now those tasks you defined can be delegated to the right people, and all you need is to communicate your vision.

SEEK AND YE SHALL FIND

I constantly think about that show *Hoarders* and the juxtaposition of the new movement around minimalism. On the series *Tidying Up with Marie Kondo*, host Marie Kondo is known to ask, "Does this thing add value to your life? Does it *spark joy*?" Identification asks the same question. Whether you're decluttering your house or reclaiming your time, the same principle applies. So ask yourself: does this task add value?

You've already devoted time to your project. You sat after the last chapter and broke it down into specialized tasks. Twenty minutes of your time created a list of smaller projects for your future team of freelancers. Now think about what comes next.

In the past, you would hurl yourself at those steps and waste hours learning new skills just to do a passable job. What if you took that same energy—and half the time— and wrote out a series of instructions for actual experts to use?

Your next task is just ahead, and I can't wait to see you on the other side. Identifying your team, your time, and your goals will open you up to a world of possibilities.

GO-DOS

Take a look at the breakout of the tasks from the Taskification exercise. Now that you better understand the various parts, it is time to explore how you might bring in expert freelancers to help you get the project completed. There was a time that I believed that all aspects of each project had to be done by me. "If I give up control, will I get credit for the work? I am the only one that can deliver with quality, right?"

Here are a few questions that I had to ask myself as I learned to collaborate with experts from around the world. Take some time and think through each of these.

1. What are your strengths? This is not an interview question, but it is something that is really important to understand as you think about identifying work where you can really have **impact**. What is your superpower?

2. What do you have fun doing? Let's be honest; you should enjoy your work. This does not mean that you can just focus on the fun parts, but think about when you feel focused and are enjoying various parts of projects.

3. Now look at the other side. What drains your energy and motivation?

4. What do you avoid doing or keep putting off? These could be tasks or parts of projects that are always on that dreaded "Should List."

5. Who can you bring in to complement your capabilities? This is a project that you are driving; think of yourself as the CEO of the project or as a director of a film. If you had the power to assemble a dream team to help you get this project across the line, what skills would fill the gaps?

6. What is your work style when working with people remotely? Do you like to jump on video calls? Would you rather have someone doing the work while you sleep? Do you want someone in the same time zone so you can collaborate in real time? Everyone has an opinion on these, so be honest.

7. If you find areas where you would want to bring in a freelancer, what information will you need to provide to ensure successful completion of the task? This will be critical when we get to talking about actual delegation.

DELEGATE

"As we look ahead into the next century, leaders will be those who empower others."

—BILL GATES, FOUNDER OF MICROSOFT

If I could teach you just one rule about delegation, it's this: you need to be willing to give up control. You need to trust others to collaborate on your vision and move toward a united goal. None of that is easy. In fact, of all the lessons and homework I've given you, this is the hardest. In order to live the Gig Mindset, to truly engage with what is possible in this new economy, you have to let others run with your ideas.

Before we even get into this chapter, I want to prime you. This is a skill you'll need to practice. Every time you sit down and start a new task, you'll get better. You'll build a network of trusted freelancers, much like you developed your current professional network.

When I talk about delegation, I'm not simply saying that you tell a freelancer what you want done. That's easy enough. Imagine you've ordered an Uber. The app allows you to plot your journey and dial in the exact spot to be dropped off. When you get in the car, you could ride the entire way in silence. Maybe, as you approach your destination, you offer a few bits of clarity to guide in those last few blocks. Think about the trust you just applied to this driver.

Could you have sat down in the passenger seat, app out, playing navigator the entire time? Sure. You could also just drive yourself if you need to have that much control. Delegation means stepping back from the driver's seat and trusting your freelancer to follow directions and ask questions if they get stuck.

Right now, I have people that do web research and data to support my arguments and narratives around a variety of topics. I have an expert who does motion graphics. I have another editor for videos. Sometimes I need graphs and charts based on the data I've sourced to support articles and newsletters. All of these tasks represent someone I've delegated to. Someone I've trusted to run with my instructions.

Instructions, as we've mentioned before, need to be written down. The act of sitting and writing and setting your expectations isn't just helpful for the freelancer; it focuses you on your outcome. I knew a small business owner who wanted a bookkeeper. She was using a traditional service that only did the basics, but she needed someone to provide reports and help with some virtual assistant tasks. She reached out and found a freelancer who could deliver exactly what she wanted for the same price, but first she had to actually take time and write down her expectations and requirements. By putting her vision down on paper, she ensured a mutual understanding with her new network.

Delegation is to assign responsibility or authority.

Responsibility is easy. When you hire someone full time, you are giving them responsibility. It's part of their job description. When you delegate to someone, you are assigning them authority. They can make decisions based on your instructions and your intent. You are trusting them to make the right choices in pursuit of a shared goal. For so many people I've met, that is the scariest thing imaginable.

I can't emphasize enough how hard that idea was for me, and still is for the people starting to work this way. We all have that expectation that we are "the only ones who can do this task." We tell ourselves that if we don't do it personally, it just won't get done. Or it won't get done *right*.

Perhaps you think this is a special skill. Remember Ken, our video editor? He thought that what he did, the videos he produced, were his defining skill. If he told someone else to do it, the result would be terrible. It wouldn't— *couldn't*—live up to his standards. Worse, if he discovered a freelancer that could do his job, that would be giving up his special skill. It would be inviting his own irrelevance.

Human beings have difficulty seeing how delegation can be a blessing. If we're honest with ourselves, it looks like a threat.

For anyone who has managed a team of people, you know the end result won't be done the same way if you do it yourself. But I'll bet you got it done. No matter the task, you and your team pulled through. And that diversity of thought made the project better. Working with a wide group of people adds new voices and perspectives and helps find new solutions to a variety of challenges.

When I engage with freelancers and bring together a wider team, I gain knowledge. My life experience is limited to my gender, my race, the neighborhood I grew up in, and the schools I attended, as well as the companies and industries where I worked. What looks "right" to me is fixed and rigid. Adding in the perspectives of people from around the world teaches me how to connect on a whole new level. It makes the market research better, designs products better, and forces me to improve my management skills and communication.

The Gig Mindset is not a shallow pond. You can't just dip in your toes, play around, and then go back to your old lifestyle. In fact, you have to come to this with a little faith, the belief that this will work. You have to lean into it, dive into the deep end with the expectation that—for just a moment—you will be completely underwater.

Trust me; you're not alone down here. In fact, these leaders all know what it's like to search for the surface.

MIKE MORRIS

Paul: Mike, what would you say to someone struggling with the concept of delegation?

Mike: The first thing, the absolute first thing, is to throw out your mentality that you have to control everything. Delegation is the opposite of micromanaging. I would say it's the "let go of control" mentality.

I think that it's a big piece of the puzzle and it takes a certain person to be able to feel comfortable with that. Most of us have grown up in a model of command and control where you were visibly seen doing something, which is the proof of you doing your job.

Everybody talks about the Industrial Revolution and how they created factories and they managed people. I mean, that's still part of our management models of current day organizations. And the ability to let go of control is something that many people are not comfortable with. It's like that article by Stephane Kasriel: We're working in twenty-first-century jobs, but we're using twentieth-century management techniques.

Corporations today are embracing remote work, letting their employees succeed based on outcomes rather than time spent sitting within walking distance of the boss' desk.

I remember when I was a young manager, I was very stressed out because I just didn't know if work was gonna get done on time. I didn't know if this person was actually gonna do their job, and it stressed me out. Every day, the same pain point. The same frustration. Because that's what not knowing does to you. It's a constant stress.

Then I figured out, "You know what? I can't control it, but I can hedge it, I can manage it." You have to go and start trusting yourself. More importantly, you have to trust others. In order to do this model, you've got to trust that this freelancer didn't grow up where you grew up. They don't live in an area like you. Heck, you might not know where they are.

You've got to be able to get comfortable with the distributed model. And for me the litmus test for that is you become fixated not on the people as much as you get fixated on the outcomes. So I don't judge. It's important to me how good a person is and what their track record is, that is important. But what really matters is the deliverable that I'm getting back. That's what matters, because everybody has good days and bad days.

All I want to know is that the deliverable that I'm getting is a good deliverable, and that's really where it stops. If you change your mindset and you focus on that, it's ultimately the better way to look at the relationship.

Let go of command and control of individuals, but focus on the quality, the workmanship, and the product of the outcome that you're getting back. It puts you in a much different mindset.

The alternative is like a lot of people that I run into in big industries. They pride themselves on the number of people that work for them. As if that number mattered in the Gig Economy. How about the number of tasks you got accomplished? How about the number of products you brought to the market?

That to me is the right way for both sides, both audiences, the producers, and the consumers.

Paul: Tie the whole process back to the outcome?

Mike: Exactly. Look, if a network of people collaborate on your vision, you get there faster together. That's what delegation gets you: results.

STEVE RADER

Paul: Steve, I have to imagine it's hard to let go of control of NASA.

Steve: I actually have a story about this. There is a project for the International Space Station (ISS) that has developed an RFID (radio-frequency identification) system to try and track the location of all of the stuff on ISS. There are thousands of items up there and it's pretty easy to lose small items in zero gravity because it can just float away on you. So, the RFID tracking system helps keep track of it all. The team has been improving the system and is currently working on finding a machine learning algorithm to more precisely track objects. The problem was that the team was having a hard time explaining the project. They eventually settled on making an explainer video, but had no idea where to start.

Our CoECI team had been working with Freelancer. com and had found that we could use the crowd to create graphics, animations, and even CAD models, and we knew that they had lots of freelancers capable of doing video work. We asked them to give us their project documents and to tell us about the project. We then handed that information off to Freelancer.com to run a storyboard contest for a three-minute video that could explain the RFID tracking project. The winner ended up being this psychologist from Australia who created this really nice story using only a set of slides. We then went on to use another contest to make the video based on her storyboard.

It was amazing for what we got for a total of about $4,500. Had we hired a production company to do that, can you imagine the invoice? A fully staffed shop running through storyboards, writing a script, animating things—that's hours and hours of skilled labor piling up. We definitely saved a few decimal places in cost.

This psychologist then went on to start bidding on other projects. We did this origami CAD challenge to give us an origami design for radiation shielding on future spacecraft. She put together a whole design, again in a slide show. Later on, however, I noticed she started submitting in CAD.

I happened to be speaking in Australia last December, and I actually got to talk with her and found out that she had learned CAD because she became so interested in these contests and wanted to be part of it, and wanted to contribute to NASA's mission. She took it even further and bought a 3D printer, because she really liked the way that worked and she thought that would be something cool. She then went on to take second place in a Grab-CAD contest that we posted to design a planetary rocks sorter. GrabCAD is made up of five million mechanical engineers and designers and she beat out all but one of them. It was crazy.

A really fascinating case study that the London Business School did a few years back: Roche Diagnostics—a large, multinational pharmaceutical company that does over $8 billion in annual R&D—was testing crowdsourced challenges to see if they worked. They took several of their unsolved problems from across their enterprise and worked with Innocentive to post them as challenges.

One of those problems was capturing the precise mea-surement of a sample's quantity and quality such that a diagnostic test could be run on that sample. Roche had worked for fifteen years to solve this problem without suc-cess. Innocentive launched a sixty-day challenge with a $20,000 prize and by the end of the challenge, they had a workable solution in two of the submissions. But the real surprise came when they looked across all of the submissions that wouldn't work and they realized that those submissions represented everything they had tried over fifteen years of proprietary research. They gathered all of it in sixty days from a crowd of around 120,000 who were not specialists in biotech. That's profound. Just the statistical possibility of them finding all of that same expertise that they had applied is just amazing.

I think it's fair to say that we don't even understand the full power of the crowd yet. It has this property, this elasticity with the right incentives and the right structures that allow you to tap into some really amazing results.

One of the changes that I think is going to happen in the next five to ten years is someone's going to figure out how to form high-performing teams in literally hours by matching up remarkable people, putting them in the right collaboration space, and handing them over to somebody to go solve a problem.

All of a sudden, we're going to get solutions like you've never seen, because that same platform could potentially spin up 150 of those high-performing teams. These types of high-performing teams already work five to six times better than normal teams. They can take on the complexities of problems that individuals can't. When you look forward, the possibility of what's to come is pretty astounding.

Paul: Dyan, you related delegation to onboarding, right?

Dyan: Engaging with a freelancer isn't all that different from delegating work to an employee. It's about trust.

Paul: How do you prepare people to let go of control and trust in their networks?

Dyan: Anyone who manages resources must think about how they recruit and onboard expert resources and delegate to those resources. Many of the methods and governance systems you would use to manage and delegate responsibilities to a full-time employee can be applied to managing a freelance expert.

To do so, as with any operations, just requires a thoughtful approach to setting priorities, recruiting great talent, defining success, equipping them with the tools they need to be successful, and then communicating and collaborating through completion. In short, define success, hire great talent, and provide them with the environment, support, and autonomy they need to be successful. Do your homework up front, empower and inspire the resources to achieve their goals, and then trust the process, trust the resources.

There are always operational controls and governance

systems in place to support the management of experts, whether they're employees or freelancers. The key is to design the work assignments and workflows in a way that best matches expertise and capacity to the desired outcome. A critical aspect of the resourcing and workflow design process is to do so in a way that best safeguards proprietary information. Important to note that the risk of potential bad behaviors are not exclusive to any one set of resources—bad actors can appear as a freelancer, as an employee, as a supplier. To delegate effectively to any resource pool, you need to maintain strong operational visibility and governance.

When I started building our gig operation GeniusLink six years ago, I believed the gig toolkit applied to heavy industrial operations could help us improve enterprise performance. I collaborated closely with our intellectual property and labor and employment teams to adopt and adapt our existing governance systems to build a scalable and compliant expert operating system. Six years later, it's clear that the GeniusLink operation has changed the paradigm.

We've enabled over $6 billion of impact for our teams and clients. We've redefined what's possible, collaborated with an incredible community of experts within and outside our company, we've inspired teams with a vision for a better way to work, and we've elevated the employee experience to help them achieve greater success.

Within the context of a noisy landscape of change, emerging technologies, new market entrants—it can be easy for professionals to compartmentalize the Gig Economy toolkit as a fad or a "nice to have." The resources within the Gig Economy are simply an expansion of the toolkit for getting work done, and they can be a path to significantly improve the outcomes of that work. The resources are not a silver bullet, they're simply a set of more precise, more digitally enabled, and potentially more efficient alternatives to connect business priorities with better outcomes—a virtually limitless, flexible portfolio of experts and solutions to drive better organizational performance.

I don't like to speak in hyperbole, but if you think about the reconfiguration of work with just these tools—the taskification and the digitization—it will allow you to create more efficient hyperlinks from problem to mission to talent to solution.

It's a living, breathing supercomputer, and all you have to do is speak the right code.

TUCKER MAX

Paul: Scribe has a large remote workforce. How do

you match the right people together and give them the responsibility of your vision?

Tucker: That's the easy part. We use written guidelines and Teamwork—a web-based collaboration software. Our model is based on assigning work and trusting our freelancers to deliver. Yeah, we have publishing managers checking in and setting milestones and deadlines, but it's a lot of the honor system too.

The hard part is getting these type A authors to connect with strangers over something as personal as a book.

Paul: I imagine that's a challenge for your authors.

Tucker: That is one of the biggest issues. We had to become masters at dealing with the psychology of high-achieving, hard-driven types of people, because we're not just asking. We are telling them, "You're not going to be in charge. You need to lose your ego for our process to work."

That is for almost everyone we work with, at least in the interview process.

We have a guided author process now, which is where you write the book yourself with our structure and guidance, and I lead that. I lead that entire program. People come, they spend two days in an office with us in a workshop.

I lead the workshop. That program is really, really good, but we just launched that about a year and a half ago, so it's still relatively new.

Most of our authors are in the interview process. It's so hard. It was one of the major problems of our company: dealing with the psychology of those people. So many of our scribes have come in and they'll look at our process and are like, "What the hell? This seems so complicated, and it seems like so many steps you don't need."

Some of them don't have a lot of experience ghostwriting, or they've only ghostwritten or done that kind of work on a one-off, casual freelance basis. They don't understand the effort that goes into managing the entire process and the psychology of the author.

Now, if they're very experienced ghostwriters, then they totally understand our process and they think it's kind of amazing. They're like, "Oh, now I get it." They've had all the bad clients or the bad client interactions.

I would say 80 percent of the problems we have with authors are not the authors. It's us setting poor expectations, or not managing expectations, or not having a process that fits, that adapts to the needs of the author while still meeting the needs of the book.

We've been a company for five years as of August 2019, and it took us at least three and a half to four years to get our process to the point where I was like, "Okay. I feel comfortable with the process."

Granted, my bar is very high. But that is really, really, really hard.

That's what my CEO does. I can't tell you how many times we've jokingly painted on his wall, "Manage expectations," or "Set expectations." He says that over and over and over again, and he's right. Because we're talking to people like you who are smart, and accomplished, and have achieved significant things, and in probably most areas of your life you go in, you're in charge, right? You know what you're doing.

From the outside, everyone thinks they can write. "Yeah, I write emails every day." Even if they don't say that consciously, subconsciously they believe they can write, and they're wrong. Almost all of them are wrong. They're terrible writers. Or even if they're good writers, they have no concept of how writing a book differs from writing an email.

You get people all the time who write fantastic blog posts, who would be good. Five hundred to 5,000 words, they're fantastic. But structuring an idea, they have no idea what to do, none. But they don't realize that.

If we don't set their expectations and then manage them, they just don't understand. They don't know what they don't know. We spend so much time on this. Over and over with calls, and repetition, and emails. All of that is about setting the proper expectations.

Dealing with a freelancer on both sides, you have to do that. Good freelancers set expectations. Most freelancers aren't good. They're not good at the act of freelancing. They're good at their skill, but they're not good at freelancing.

I can't tell you how many writers that we have, either full time or part time, that work for us at anywhere from 50 to 90 percent off their normal quoted rate. The reason is because we take all of the business of freelancing off their plate. They don't need to find clients. They don't need to worry about managing the clients other than doing the work. They don't need to worry about money. They don't need to worry about any of the bullshit. All they have to do is show up and bring their skills. That's a huge part of what we provide, a benefit to them.

When you're building your team, when you're pushing your tasks on them, that's what you have to keep in mind.

That's what will separate you from all the other people fumbling around with freelancers. Set expectations. Manage expectations. And communicate clearly what you need.

Paul: And then trust in your network.

DO THIS, NOT THAT

The number one challenge, the number one place where people struggle, is communication. I've seen it from thousands of people. They finish my lectures and they're excited. This new mindset is going to change their lives. They pick a task and they can't wait to get started. Breaking tasks down into specific steps? Too easy. Identifying experts? They're all over the place! Then it comes time to delegate, and everything screeches to a halt.

They struggle with how to communicate their expectations to someone who may not have shared context; to give up control and trust. Years back, I did an experiment and gave a number of people access to my virtual assistant. I was walking with one of my friends who was trying this out and asked how she was using the service. She said, "I do not know what to delegate; I have never had an assistant."

Now they have to articulate those tasks. They have to provide specific instructions and then just walk away. For a lot of people, this is new. It's easy to sit in a meeting and just talk, but far more difficult when you have to write a descriptive project brief to delegate.

It's understandable. Your tasks are so innate to you. If you closed your eyes, you could picture every detail. Now you have to work with someone who doesn't share that context, and you have to place all your hopes and expectations into them. It's a real learning process.

Delegation isn't just saying, "Go do this." It's building expectations, setting timelines, and really engaging with these experts. It is getting your vision on paper with examples of things that inspire you. It's trusting that they are professionals and want to deliver the very best. Most of all, it's about having an open and curious mind throughout the process.

I've seen people go overboard. Some are so specific that they don't give their expert the freedom to work. Some are so vague that they might as well not have said anything at all. I have also seen people be unrealistic on delivery times, not giving space for collaboration. Remember, this takes practice. Do not expect to be great at this out of the gate. Leave room for trial and error. I'll give you an example: you need to cater a working lunch for a group of ten.

Now, if you were to just ask a virtual assistant to find a place to eat, you'd get back a pretty bland response. Maybe something in their list would fit your needs, but it would be a roll of the dice. What about dietary restrictions or allergies for the other people? You've provided too little information and context to expect a good result.

If you asked a coworker or friend to recommend a restaurant, you could trust the results. My friends know me; we share the context of enjoyed meals. If I asked this question, I'd get back a few options for Japanese BBQ (it's delicious, and that's the only culinary advice I'm providing in this book). Their recommendations are based on the context and shared experiences built over the years. Freelancers— unless you've worked with them before—don't have that shared knowledge. You have to direct them.

So you go back to the freelancer, but you ask a more detailed question: "I'd like somewhere to order lunch. It needs to be within fifteen miles of my office, my boss prefers Italian, and it needs to be vegan-friendly. Also, we are capped at $30 a person."

You've provided the same request but with context. You want something specific, but not so specific that the request is redundant. If I engaged a virtual assistant and said, "I'd like to eat at McDonald's tonight," I've wasted our time and my money.

Honestly, delegation took me a while to perfect. I had to train myself, and I made mistakes early on. I'm sharing those with you now so you don't have to start at square one. Use my knowledge, and the stories from our panel, to set yourself up for success.

CAN'T SOMEONE ELSE DO IT

Let's talk about the problem. You had a goal, right? Something you had on that "Should List" that you finally decided to do. Then you broke it down into tasks. Oh man, that just made things better. It made it simpler, seeing the easy small steps. But the same problem from before crept up: Time.

So you found experts in the world, people who could take on those tasks. These freelancers had the skills and the drive to execute your step-by-step list, to help you achieve your goal. This is great. Only now you've got a team. This "Should List" was once personal. If it failed, the only person losing out was you. Now there's a group involved, more eyeballs on the prize, and suddenly it feels overwhelming. This feeling can be stronger at work. Imagine your team and your boss are waiting on deliverables. You feel stuck.

Radical delegation is about practice. Start delegating with small tasks, which leads you to more complex tasks. It is all about your relationship with time. You have to go back and look at all the tasks for this project. What are the trade-offs? What has to go? No matter what you do in life, your time is finite. Whether you work in the mailroom or the top-floor corner office, you have the same number of hours in a day. You can't do everything you want. You can't even do all the tasks you *need* to do, at least not alone. So you need to start looking at your life and selecting those items you can delegate out. What can you give up, relinquish all control of, so you can have more time and space?

I felt this way. My panel felt this way. We looked at our lives, our work, and our families, and we saw that there just wasn't enough of us to go around. I want to work, to make an impact, but I also want to spend time with my family. When you start practicing the Gig Mindset, you'll see a new possibility.

That's why you need to start small. Radical delegation doesn't come overnight. You build to it over many smaller projects.

Start small. Do a couple of projects in the virtual system. Engage with a virtual assistant on one of the platforms and practice giving detailed instructions. You're not writing pages and pages of notes, just a few bulleted guidelines.

Giving up control is hard, but it gets easier as you build your trusted network of freelancers. The goal is to find your tribe. After a while, you will see that your value isn't the control. Your value comes with the exponential opportunities you create by engaging with these experts. Ken the editor went from a few videos a month to forty. His value actually increased by allowing experts to take on many of the tasks required to create his innovative videos. Think about what you could do with the extra time created by the Gig Mindset.

Do you have a special project you want to do at work? Or a family activity that keeps being pushed back? Or a trip to visit family and friends? Reclaiming your time unleashes the power of possibility, and that comes from delegation.

If you think this is radical as an individual, imagine what it can do for you as a manager. The old boss mentality was simple. You showed up, sat in the high chair at meetings, barked orders from your office, and provided your "wisdom" to your employees.

When you empower your employees to use the Gig Mindset, you add a force multiplier to your team. Each person becomes an engine of activity, bringing in expertise that you couldn't have expected before. I did this with my team, and I can tell you it wasn't easy. I had to give up control, kill the micromanager, and lean into the idea of complete empowerment. After a while, I really started believing and empowering people, trusting them to do their work. In many ways, I just became a sounding board for these new experts, unblocking their path however I could.

I reset my defaults. I evolved. When I told you this was going to be radical change, I wasn't kidding. You've heard from the experts; you've learned from my mistakes. Now it's time to challenge yourself.

GO-DOS

This is where the rubber hits the road and is often the hardest part of implementing the T.I.D.E. Model. It has taken me a long time to get good at the art of radical delegation, and I am still learning new skills every day. Below are some questions that you will want to ask as you get ready to engage with an expert freelancer on a project. This is also good practice when working with any remote team.

1. What are your project/task deliverables? Are they clearly thought out and written down? The number one change for many people is that they need to start documenting their expectations and specifics around the expected outcome. (Pro tip: take a walk and record your thoughts via your phone and then have them transcribed by a freelancer. A quick edit and you have start.)

2. What are your schedules and deadlines? These are critical to understand. As you get started, make sure that you leave time to build a working relationship. You are learning how to work in a new way, and the freelancer is learning how best to deliver the task.

3. What does your job/task/project look like when it is done *well*? I always advise starting from the end result and working backward. You have the vision in

your mind, so take some time to articulate it when you write up the deliverables. The more specific, the easier it is.

4. Describe how this task/project fits in the big picture, in the vision/larger/broader business goals. One of the biggest hurdles to overcome when starting to work with freelancers is making sure that everyone has a shared context. I always work to articulate up front. As I worked through this book, I engaged a ton of amazing freelancers for research help. I always let them know that the work was for a book, and I provided a one-page summary that had the context of what I wanted to publish. This helped everyone get on the same page and provided for great research.

5. Write up your communication plan—method and frequency. I mentioned this in the Identify section—most people either forget this part or just assume you will figure it out as you go along. In my experience this is a mistake. *How* you work is critical to ensuring a trusted working relationship, high-quality deliverables, and ability to hit timelines successfully. This includes how you want to be updated so that you do not fall into the trap of micromanagement.

6. Provide constructive feedback (and ask for feedback) throughout the process—and be specific. Explain how

and why you do a task a certain way, and how it ties into the end goal.

7. What are you afraid of letting go or losing control of? As you finish this section, think about those fears. Ask yourself why you have them and push to see if there are more opportunities to delegate to an expert free-lancer.

EVOLVE

"The best way to predict the future is to invent it."

—ALAN KAY, APPLE'S CHIEF SCIENTIST

The first step of change is admitting there is a problem. You wake up one day, look around, and realize that your life isn't what you want it to be. You're stuck, and the world is moving faster around you. Business changed, the way we live and work changed, and you're standing still. You have to evolve if you're going to get out of the quicksand.

The increasing pace of technology means adapting and adopting are the only options. It is critical to reskill, and "Evolve" is about that reskilling.

My movement into the Gig Mindset took time. I experimented every single day, playing with tasks and projects and hobbies until the system made sense. I broke down my Should List into specific tasks, identified the expert help I needed, and delegated the work to freelancers with the space and skillset to do what I couldn't. In those weeks and months, I saw the power of the Gig Economy in action. My workload decreased and my output increased exponentially. I discovered a power to make more of an impact than I ever could alone.

I started doing projects that I had only dreamed possible: writing the articles that have been in my head; doing research on a wide variety of topics; and publishing the book you are holding in your hand. All of this with a full-time job, a family, and time for myself.

The momentum kept growing. My confidence and trust in my network allowed me to try more complex tasks. One task led to the next. It was like in a video game. My skills improved, which allowed me to unlock the next level, which allowed my skills to improve even more.

You need to evolve, to fully adapt into a new lifestyle. Each interaction teaches you something, so you need to lean in and listen. Learn what you can do to evolve, to be better in the practice of the Gig Mindset. When you're struggling with a diet, you go to a fitness instructor. When you have a medical concern, you go to a doctor. When your career is stagnant or toxic, what do you do? I'm amazed at how few people reach out and try career coaches.

If you recall all the way back in the introduction, I've used career coaches. More than one! They are invaluable people to have in your life.

Demand that help at work. Your company has put a lot of time and resources into molding you into a valuable employee. They are invested in your success. They want to provide you with the tools to level up because that means more productivity.

A few years ago, Ken the video editor and I were sitting at a table discussing how to overcome the challenges that people have when starting to engage with freelancers on various projects. The conversation turned to the evolution we were seeing in the Gig Economy. Suddenly, Ken stood up and marched to the front of the room. He grabbed a dry erase marker and scrawled "No More All-Nighters" across the whiteboard.

We both stopped. It was like one of those scenes in an inspirational movie. We'd been dancing around the thought all day, and Ken simply put it into perspective. What we wanted, what we all hoped to gain through this change in the workplace, wasn't just about finding free-lancers. It wasn't about outcomes. It was an evolution of what work could be. No more all-nighters.

The Gig Mindset isn't about how to get busier. You're

already busy. There are dozens and dozens of books out there about how to keep yourself jumping from task to task, managing your emails, stuck in the Busy Trap. What I'm telling you is that you can reclaim more control by giving up some of that busy work. Reclaim your time. Evolve.

Elon Musk set out not to build a faster car but to change the world; a new car just happened to be a step in that process. Tesla went and threw everything out the window. They started from the ground up and built something no one had ever seen before.

When Satya came to Microsoft, he had literally written the book *Hit Refresh* about the changing dynamic of the workplace.

Bill Gates had a great quote: "People overestimate what they can do in a year, and underestimate what they can do in ten." Change comes slowly. I wake up every day and try something new. It's baby steps. I'm crawling toward the newest, best version of myself. At the same time, I look back at where I was just a few years ago, and I'm amazed at how far I've come.

Evolution is about changing what you are, slowly and methodically. Don't just take it from me. Our panel went through that same struggle, and they emerged on the other side shiny and new.

MIKE MORRIS

Paul: We're talking about evolution, about the changing landscape. What have you seen at Topcoder?

Mike: I mean number one, there's a couple of macro themes that we're seeing at the same time.

One is we're seeing the freelance industry explode, and it's exploding from the workers' side. I mean that's a true trend. People are choosing to be freelancers at a much higher rate than they were years ago.

You can go through all the studies. I think in our industry, over 50 percent of the people are choosing freelancing as their means of getting their income versus traditional. That's a huge trend, but it's still not correctly being covered. The US government economic reports don't effectively track freelancers in the Gig Economy, and it's a big impact on our economy.

I think that's an issue, but that's one big trend that we're seeing that's going to continue.

The trend is happening without a lot of the core underlying problems being solved. Things like: How do we provide retirement security for people that are career gig workers? How do we provide health care and other benefits normally found in traditional workplaces? How do we enable gig workers to survive?

Those problems will be solved with time, and by companies like Topcoder that are looking to solve them. When those problems become less of an issue, the rate of people choosing freelancing over traditional jobs is just going to grow.

When I graduated college, the only people I knew freelancing were the ones that couldn't find a real job. It's drastically different now. I advise a lot of people, and sometimes I'm like, "You know what? Just get a normal job for a little bit just so you see what that's like, and try freelancing." The Gig Economy is so attractive that there are freelancers who have never worked a traditional job before.

I found myself saying to people, "Just see what it's like to work regular hours. You may want to be able to go out for happy hours and stuff like that, get that experience, and then go do freelancing." I feel like a parent advising their child to at least try the college experience.

It's a big difference from ten, twenty years ago.

The second thing is AI: artificial intelligence. AI is a huge trend, as is the digitization of the workplace. When you start to take traditional business processes and put them into a platform, you are digitizing them. You're taking them from analog and you're putting them into the cloud.

It allows you to now apply AI to those processes. You can't apply AI to a vinyl record, but you can to an MP3 and it's the same model here. We're gonna see AI advancements in a number of ways. When we run out of our 50x capacity in seven months, we'll find a way to squeak out an extra 30 percent to 40 percent capacity by automating the process. It hasn't yet become a bottleneck for us, but it's on our road map.

We're seeing these changes in our process today. I had a call with our CTO recently, and we were talking about how quickly technology has evolved. I know, it sounds like two old-timers yearning for the good old days. That's how fast tech moves now. You can be thirty-five and still find yourself behind the technological curve.

Five or seven years ago, people thought you were nuts if you said cars were going to drive themselves. Well they are driving themselves. Today. AI is able to manage rudimentary workloads around software development, design, and data science. Areas like setting up the data, finding the data, analyzing the data, scoping how big a piece of work is, deploying processes into cloud environments, and managing those cloud environments. That's not nearly as complicated as driving down my street and stopping.

AI has huge longevity for us that's going to be really impactful in all industries.

The third thing is this: You need to be aware of the evolution of cloud technology.

It's like every incremental step that the cloud makes is a 10x step that the crowdsourcing economy can make. You think about business models today, Uber is not possible without the smartphone. Likewise, the Gig economy is not possible without cloud infrastructure.

Just think about Topcoder. We have thousands of development environments, so it'd be impossible for us to manage that with the old physical infrastructure. But we can manage it within Azure, we can manage it within AWS within seconds and clicks of a button.

And then every time the cloud does the next thing—they go and they do server-free computing—well guess what? You just made our job 10x easier again. Every evolution of the cloud is hugely impactful, so as technology advances we're going down a path that's becoming more prone to Gig Economy-style business models, to virtual labor models.

This new model isn't going anywhere. Five years from now, people aren't going to be programming on a mainframe sitting inside one office in McLean, Virginia. It's not going that direction, it's going as far away from that direction as humanly possible, which is enabling this more.

If you want to keep up with the Gig Economy, if you want to be a part of the movement rather than left behind, you need to understand these three trends. You need to evolve.

STEVE RADER

Paul: One part of the tech evolution that fascinates me is artificial intelligence.

Steve: Oh, absolutely. AI is everywhere—selecting your music and organizing the traffic in your city. You probably have a dozen apps on your phone right now that are driven by artificial intelligence.

Paul: Do you think someone can maintain their relevance if they don't evolve?

Steve: The short answer is "no." From big technological changes to smaller organizational ones, the rules are simple: Evolve or die. Okay, maybe that's a bit of a stretch, but you can't keep thinking the same way. You can't keep *doing* it the same way.

I'm reminded of a contest we ran. A major potato chip

company was using a crowdsourced challenge to solve a problem that was age-old: *How do we get grease off potato chips without breaking them?* Their best solution at the time was to vibrate the tray of chips as it came out of a vat of oil. The chips had slightly less oil and was deemed more palatable, but a significant percentage of those chips would break.

Food production is largely staffed with mechanical engineers who are trained in mechanical vibration and are the people you go to if you have a vibration problem. You see that reflected in the original chip solution—just vibrate the chip.

But that approach left a lot of broken chips and damaged inventory. That's money literally thrown away at the end of the day. So how do you fix it? How do you solve a problem when you've already gone to the experts and they've *technically* solved it?

Well, you approach the problem in a different way. First, they changed their problem statement from: *"How do you get the grease off potato chips?"* to *"How do you remove a viscous fluid from a delicate wafer?"* This opened up the problem to more than just food production engineers. If you'd just said, "How do I get grease off potato chips?" the only people that are going to be interested in that are those that are likely to have already been working the problem. As soon as you say, "How do you remove viscous fluid from a delicate wafer?" that opens you up to more experts. Is it silicon wafers? Is it something having to do with biotech? It becomes a broader physics question. You just cast a wider net, and as we've seen chapter after chapter, diversity of thought breeds innovation.

It ended up that the solution was to acoustically vibrate the *air* around the chip at the natural frequency of the oil. The oil just flies off the chip and doesn't break it. You might not even be an expert in vibration and are probably thinking to yourself, *Oh yeah, that makes total sense.*

Here's the thing. It was still a vibration solution and the existing experts should have seen that, but for some reason, they remained blind to it.

Instead, the solution is rumored to have come from a violinist who had seen the rosen vibrate off her bow when she played certain musical notes. She understood what natural frequency was and that kind of visual experience led her to make this submission.

Kind of fascinating, right? It's unexpected diversity, but it also points out that within a discipline there is a shell of "you don't know what you don't know." There's this boundary between what's possible and what you know. Even within a discipline like mechanical engineering where they should have seen such an obvious solution. I mean, how could they not?

If physical vibration was selected in the production design, why hadn't acoustic vibration been considered? For many years they missed that. I think that people working in a given domain can be blind to certain ideas and often don't see some of the amazing innovations going on in other domains that may be just the thing they need for their problem. Those are the people that can really benefit from the crowd. They can go to the crowd to find an idea that they missed or have been blind to or maybe find a skill, expertise, or technology from some other sector. These are the crucial ingredients to find and take back into the lab to develop the innovative solutions necessary to stay competitive.

That's what this new economy needs, and that requires an innovative mind. As Paul says, you have to reset your defaults and make the new normal. Technology is only going to grow faster. It's evolving, so you need to as well.

Paul: And what does that mean to you?

Steve: Simply put, you can't stay stuck in one place, or one mindset. You can't think, "Oh, well this has worked for me up until now. It'll probably keep working forever." Don't be afraid to try something radical, something innovative. Always believe that there is a better way and seek it out.

Paul: I think the misconception is that evolution is only personal. Dyan, you've seen evolution happen in heavy industry, right?

Dyan: I know it's a little bit of a hyperbole, but these new business models that are enabled by the Gig Economy really allow us to challenge the status quo. We can challenge our perceptions of what's possible, open up the landscape of what we can achieve and how we can achieve it by removing some of the boundaries between our team and the rest of the world.

2014 was really the year where we got our gig legs underneath us so to speak. We were operating under a very similar set of guiding principles. We developed a playbook that would allow us to create effective, compliant, and scalable hyperlinks between our missions and the best talent and solutions. We didn't have the benefit of the blueprint, the T.I.D.E Model. The introduction of Paul's model has been a brilliant synthesis of how to "get gig right"—it helps organizations get started with Gig Economy resources, and to scale their adoption of the tools.

Back in 2014, we were generating a great portfolio of experience with the Gig Economy, freelancers, and open innovation. We were able to run a lot of experiments and projects across all of the industries that we served. I intentionally selected projects and programs across every business function and in every industry that we serve to see if I could test the boundaries of what worked with Gig Economy tools, what wouldn't work, where, and to what effect. By managing a diverse portfolio of programs, we also developed a great process for work and resource design. In any given program, we would optimize outcomes with thoughtful scope definition, requirements articulation, competency taxonomy, expert recruitment and engagement, workflow design, and knowledge and asset transfer.

Basically, we had dialed in the macro and micro-movements of work that enabled us to very effectively reach beyond the constraints of our traditional resource base to a virtually limitless pool of talent and solutions—augmenting the reach of our human resourcing and sourcing, and improving the agility and performance of our operations.

So some teams would augment their strategic work, others would augment tactical work. In some cases we would work on a discrete project, in other cases we would work on a collection of projects. But the blueprint approach enabled us to deploy gig experts and methodology—the toolkit—across every business and function and help teams around the world leverage the approach with confidence.

2014 was when we really increased our portfolio of programs and scaled the application of these methodologies across the entire enterprise. When I heard about the blueprint from Paul, that just became one of our go-to references, because Paul has done such a beautiful job of synthesizing and simplifying the playbook for people to really easily wrap their heads around.

The first example we'll walk through is one of the more heavyweight industrial examples that we have in our portfolio. This example relates to our objective to improve the operations of some of our factories around the world. We always have the opportunity to leverage new capabilities, technologies, and business models to improve production performance. And with the onset of the internet of things and additive manufacturing capabilities—we've been able to rethink production operations to take full advantage of the capabilities, connecting minds with machines for better production performance.

I mean, Henry Ford came up with a brilliant way to build a car, but that was a hundred years ago. We've learned a thing or two.

Factory planning, as you might imagine, is pretty vast and complex. There are a lot of capabilities out there that are available to improve the productivity of manufacturing operations, and so the ability to quantify the impact of various workflows, technologies and capabilities can make a big difference between a successful deployment of brilliant factory operations and one that can be very expensive and less than optimal.

In this example, one of our European teams established a plan to optimize operations in a number of production sites around the world. The team had limited capacity and an ambitious plan—they needed the support of additional, highly specialized resources to get the job done.

Taskification enabled this team to more effectively compartmentalize everything that needed to get done, and greater freedom in selecting which experts would be assigned to each task or deliverable. The team knew this approach would enable them to drive a successful outcome, with limited resources against the very complex challenge of optimizing a lot of different plant profiles. By taskifying the work, the team knew that it would be most helpful for their broader objective if they could engage a resource or resources that could help them conduct a highly specialized simulation process to analyze and quantify the options that were available: optimizing manufacturing operations and delivering credible recommendations that they could take to their leadership to prioritize the investments—in manufacturing operations around the world.

Taskification gave the team the freedom to break down

their goal—which was very strategic and extensive—into component tasks to determine which tasks they should deliver with the resources on their own team, and which tasks would be better delivered by an expert recruited from Gig Economy talent markets. This greater freedom in sourcing highly specialized experts and solutions, and the greater precision afforded by taskification, meant the team could dramatically improve performance.

To break it down further: To make the best use of available resources, the team identified the tasks that needed to be done by the expert resources—the gig resources—and the competencies that would drive the best results. The scope of the tasks included the development of manufacturing simulation models and scenario and impact assessments. We recruited experts that were fit to the task and who collaborated extremely well with the team.

The team began the effort by modeling two factories: one in China, and one in Germany. We asked the expert resource to help us model and simulate different capabilities and production options for those two sites.

For the China site, this expert leveraged used a 3D process simulation software to evaluate new production lines. The assessment focused on line design and work combinations to factor in new capabilities and optimize production performance.

So the simulation and optimization process was focused on the identification of a potential manufacturing configuration that would be difficult and time consuming to develop with traditional design methods. With the highly specialized competency of the expert we recruited, and the new simulation modeling capabilities that he had experience with and access to, the team was now able to accelerate and expand their options analysis, and quantify the potential benefit of their configuration recommendation for that particular plant.

And for the site in Germany, the expert worked with the team using simulation software to create an integrated model of multiple production lines and the associative material logistics, picking processes to run various scenarios and determine the best configuration and to drive the greatest possible performance.

This isn't a simple process. The simulations are deeply unintuitive and require time to skill into. The benefit of using them is completely wasted if you don't know what you're doing. This expert, the gig resource, brought a depth of expertise that opened up the door for an entirely new way to validate the plan options.

With thoughtful work design through taskification, and thoughtful resource design through Gig Economy resourcing methodology, the team was able to achieve much greater success than they could have achieved with a simply traditional approach to work and resourcing. They were able to run a number of simulations for both sites, based on the additional capabilities and capacity the expert brought to the table. He was able to run a multitude of options to help them make better decisions regarding optimal plant configuration, flow and automation selections—driving the greatest possible economic benefit for those two sites. This also provided a flexibility to accommodate additional future technology investments for those two sites.

That was a really successful deployment of a fairly sophisticated gig resource assignment. They were so successful, in fact, that that expert has been engaged by our teams on a number of similar site optimization projects—we'll typically run a handful of those very advanced modeling efforts each year for various manufacturing sites. This team has a consistent pipeline of production optimization efforts that ladder up to their strategic advanced manufacturing goals.

That was where we thought our expert operating system methodology method would take us. The truth is that engaging with gig resources required an evolution of our own mindsets and behaviors. We generally rely on gig resources—experts—to bring in the latest skills, tech, and software. Similarly, our teams have to provide the experts with the opportunity, governance framework, and operating freedom so we can both see the best advantages.

As Paul says, this new mindset requires evolution. Keeping up with the times. It is about bringing a new and diverse set of thinking and experiences to solve hard problems. This is a complete change in mindset for many frontline workers, managers, and companies.

TUCKER MAX

Paul: Tucker, for as long as you've been at this, what is one of the most enduring myths about evolution that you've seen?

Tucker: That it's a myth. That evolution is something that happens to other people, or other industries. If you're the dude sitting on the Titanic thinking, "Well, *my* section hasn't sunk yet," you're in for a rude awakening.

I see it in the publishing industry all the time. It's why Scribe is constantly moving, changing, growing. There are so many smart people here whose sole job is making sure we stay ahead of the trends.

Evolution is natural, it's normal. It's how industries stay alive for a hundred years. Amazon started selling books, and then they evolved when they saw the opportunities on the market. We all got used to taxis and car services, and then Uber showed up and invited us into some stranger's car.

Scribe's model works now because of the Gig Economy. There are so many talented experts out there, waiting to be tapped, and we built a company around it.

Paul: So what keeps people from evolving? What gives them that fear to try something new?

Tucker: You know what it is? Most people judge *themselves* by their intentions and *other people* by their actions.

Like, we have so many authors who they feel like they're a good person and they think they're doing good things, even though they're messing the workflow up for us left, right, and center, because they're judging themselves by their intentions.

We have freelancers who will do that as well as full-time people. What we have to train our people to do is to judge themselves by the same standard that they judge others, right?

The way you reframe that is you judge yourself by your actions, and you interpret everyone else's actions in the most charitable possible intention. Look at what they're doing and say, "Why do they think this is a good thing to do?"

They could be wrong, right? Because God knows I've done something and thought, "Oh, I didn't know that was going to turn out that way." We all do. But if you look at it that way, then it's much, much easier to understand where the intersection of communication is breaking down.

It helps to create a framework, a path forward, and the best thing to do is set expectations up front. "I'm going to do this, you're going to do that, and together we will accomplish our goal." So many people set expectations for the other person, but not for themselves, and that's where you lose traction. That's where the outcome gets lost. Set expectations and boundaries and measurables for both sides, and then make sure both sides keep each other accountable.

What does it all mean? It means that to grow, to change, to make any kind of impact, you have to set and hold the standard. It's easy when it's just you, alone in your house, messing around on the computer. When you're talking about a team of people relying on you for guidance, that's hard. That's where people get scared.

Taskify. Easy. Break it down, but know what the hell you

want. Be specific. Identify, and don't forget to vet and train these new people in how you want them to work. Delegate, and be laser focused in your design.

Do that and you'll evolve. You'll grow. It's like working out. If you wake up every day and run ten miles, you're guaranteed to lose weight and get in crazy shape. If you wake up and walk ten feet, don't expect anything to change.

JOHN WINSOR

Paul: Evolution can be a daily exercise, as John has seen firsthand.

John: I take an Uber every time I go to the airport. Three Ubers ago, a guy was driving me from Boulder to the terminal. So about a mile from the drop-off point, he turned off the ride. And I asked him, "Well, why did you do that?"

He told me, "Well, if I turn off the ride now, then I can get a ride right when I drop you off. But if I turn off when I drop you off, then I have to go out to the parking lot and wait two hours in a queue." And I thought it was super cool to see somebody that had the curiosity to figure out a more efficient way, a very entrepreneurial perspective.

So to test that, the last two rides I've told that story to the Uber drivers, and each of the Uber drivers didn't believe me. And then they did the same action of turning it off. And sure enough, within two or three seconds, they got another ride. I think that's what entrepreneurs do really, really well. They see a system and they figure out a way to hack it to make it more efficient. And those are the people that I always want on my teams and my companies.

How do we make this better for everybody? How can we get work done in a more efficient way, and fulfill the needs of our customers? You have to ask those questions and be honest about your answers if you're going to evolve.

I'm reminded of a story from the SIA conference a while back. Someone was talking about leveling up your output. They said it's not about taking an internal employee that writes one hundred lines of code a day to an external employee that writes one hundred lines of code a day. The real success is going to be when you take the hundred lines of code from an internal employee and engage a superhuman freelancer that's figured out how to write code with AI, that could write ten million lines of code a day.

That's the endgame. That's evolution. We're not trying to outsource; we're trying to explore the limits of our productivity. That's the mindset Paul is developing.

PRACTICE THE PRACTICAL

If you spent fifteen minutes on something new every single day, how much could you get done? If you broke it down into normal work hours, you'd have eleven extra working days spent on your new skill.

It's the same idea behind any lifestyle change. If I told you to wake up and jog for fifteen minutes a day, pretty soon you'd be running five or ten miles. Give it more time, and suddenly you're signing up for marathons. The change came slowly, but it came through persistence. It came with evolution and being truly curious about what I could learn.

If you went back to 1999 and told me where I would end up, I wouldn't believe you. I was stuck in my old mindset. From the time I started at Dell, the path was to work hard and get promoted—not reinventing myself professionally. I was sitting through tons of meetings but did not feel empowered to change. I didn't *want* to change back then. I didn't think I needed to. Heck, when I was living through this evolution, I had concerns. I fought my instincts. I felt my bad habits rear up and try to reclaim control. What I am now versus where I was is a radical shift.

The truth is that I needed to change. I didn't realize it was an option until suddenly it was the only option. When I saw my days slipping away meeting after meeting, I knew I needed to change. When I watched my daughters playing outside while I worked on a slideshow, I knew I needed to change. When I felt my skills would not keep me relevant in the future, I needed to change.

The T.I.D.E. Model came together as I thought about all the great revolutions in the workplace. Henry Ford changed the way we build cars, and Elon Musk changed the way we think of cars. I looked around and realized we'd been working the same way for decades, and there was a better way. I saw that I could use the changing economy to reclaim what I'd lost. I needed to reskill, to evolve, in order to keep up with the disruptions all around me.

At this point in the book, I'll bet you're pretty fired up. I hope you are. If you've been sticking to the tasks at the end of each chapter, you've already accomplished more than you'd expected. Passion projects from your Should List are now on the worktable. They're moving forward. These are just the first steps in your journey, and it only gets better from here.

Evolution is tricky. It's difficult. It requires patience, time, and determination. You have to fight against the urge to slide backward toward that old comfort. Trust me. When you see what the Gig Mindset makes possible, you'll never want to do work the old way again.

GO-DOS

For me, this has been the most exciting part of my journey into the Gig Mindset. What started as trying to reclaim time with my family has turned into radically transforming the way I live and work. Each interaction, each project has taught me new things about myself and pushed me out of my comfort zone (in a good way). I have been exposed to a diversity of thought from around the world, and this new way of "working with curiosity" has made me open to change. Here are a few thoughts to reflect on after you have completed a few projects.

1. What are three to five items that were really challenging as you worked through the T.I.D.E Model? I am sure you could write a longer list, but focus on three to five for now. Next to each, write your key learning and what you could do in the future to be better?

2. What are the other areas of your life or work where you could engage with expert freelancers to help you scale your efforts at home, work, or side/passion projects?

3. What are some new habits that could help you as you think about evolving? What are some small actions you can take as you embrace the Gig Mindset? You are now on a journey and making adjustments along the way will be critical. This will feel different as most of your life may have been focused on the destination.

4. Build your network and celebrate your successes. One of the most inspiring results of the work that I do is when someone reaches out to share an amazing story about a freelancer who changed their perception of what is possible! As you go through this process, reach out to friends, coworkers, and others (send me a message on LinkedIn) and share your experience. Building a support network and sharing best practices is a critical step in evolving your mindset.

MAKING THE
ELEPHANT DANCE

"The greatest danger in times of turbulence is not the turbulence—it is to act with yesterday's logic."

—PETER DRUCKER

It's not easy being a trendsetter. No matter how confident you are, there will always be people in your circle ready to nitpick and question the new you. When you're on a diet, people will bombard you with their own tips and tricks and questions and concerns. When you're starting an exercise regimen, people will undercut your success with their own hang-ups.

The same is true with the Gig Mindset: not attending meetings, people saying that you are just being disruptive and not "getting with the program," pushing against the way things are done. That makes people uncomfortable.

This is a change to the norm: remote working, documenting projects up front, building a trusted network, embracing being uncomfortable. From the outside, it might look a little crazy. I'll bet you thought so when you first picked up this book. Hey, who is this guy named Paul talking about shaking up the way I work?

Making the elephant dance means making this whole process work. How do you get people on board with the new you? How do you convince them that there is something special about this way of working, that the model is sound? How do you spread the love and build a team of like-minded doers?

Well, the first tool you have is in your hands right now. Lend them a copy of this book. If I've done my job and convinced you, then the preceding pages worked as intended. Aim me at your coworkers and let me loose.

The biggest hurdles people adopting this mindset face, time and again, are the various myths about the new economy and gig workers. People have horror stories about working with freelancers, tasking out work, or trying to reskill to stay relevant. They don't believe that things can really change, or that change can really bring them the life they want. They don't believe it because they've been fed a steady stream of half-truths, or they've been given the wrong information by well-meaning friends.

That's your real obstacle to success.

There are so many bogus myths out there. I come across the same few all the time: Freelancers don't do good work; they miss deadlines; they're not shaving every day. All of that is wrong (except maybe the last one). All of that comes from the fear of getting overwhelmed by change. It's a fear that, oddly enough, you can overcome only by changing. By evolving. By resetting your defaults and recognizing the truth of your current situation.

It's like buying a new pair of shoes. They may not fit at first, but you just need to take time to break them in.

In order to make this work, you need to understand the truth of what the Gig Mindset brings to the table. Thankfully, my expert panel stuck around for one more chapter just to help you succeed.

This entire book is based on more than just my belief that the concept works. The mindset works because I've been living it, because I've seen others transform by living it, and the proof is in the pudding. This isn't just some guy named Paul ranting from cover to cover. You've heard stories from Topcoder, from NASA, and from GE. This is just the tip of the iceberg. Hundreds of companies and *millions* of freelancers work this way every day. This model can be successful across a number of disciplines. All it needs is you and your effort.

MIKE MORRIS

Paul: Why are so many people caught up in the myths around engaging with freelancers?

Mike: It's a resistance to change. It's typically, in my opinion, stemming from a resistance to change and a fear of change. A fear of risk that the change brings.

One fear I hear a lot is about bringing in outsiders into the company. Fear of these strangers getting their hands on IP.

Intellectual property (IP) is something people jump to and I can argue it; I can shut an IP lawyer down on this. You're gonna tell me that having a badge and walking into a building—that's more secure than being able to track every piece of data that goes from one node to another node, and who touches it, who's allowed to touch it, who can download it, and who cannot download it?

I mean there's no possibility of walking outside of our development environments with a laptop, or a Zip disk, or a USB Drive. You cannot, it is not allowed, and, in fact, I can tell what you did when you were in there, and you

can't tell. When I walked into a major company's building two weeks ago, they can't tell what I did. A badge
doesn't protect against that. Software does. Modern
controls do.

It's just based on very archaic views of the world and the
same thing comes with security. You can have security
infused into everything.

For example: We have a piece of code that goes out to a
freelancer. We check it to make sure that it doesn't have
any proprietary information in it. Not only do we man-
ually check it; we also have software that checks it, very
sophisticated scanning software that checks it. When
the code comes back in it goes through another set of
very sophisticated inspections, every single piece of code,
even a bug fix to a piece of code.

Whereas in a traditional methodology you don't think
about things at that level, at every transaction level, at
every interaction level. And when you put those items in
a platform, and you digitize them, you go from vinyl to
digital. You now have the ability to enforce things like IP,
and security, and quality at such a minute level, you can't
come close to it the traditional way.

I could spend all day debunking this myth. By the end
of it, I'd prove to you that this is more secure than any-

thing you're doing, and you'd probably call in question everything you've been doing today. So the resistance to change is my ultimate point.

That fear of change is ugly, and you have to watch for it. I liken it to a grim reaper that is in people's minds when they think of the Gig Economy. "What does it mean to my job? What does it mean to the job of the people that work for me that make me important every day? What does it mean for the future?"

These fears *feel* real.

The analogy Paul has been using is comfort food. I think people eat a lot of comfort food all the time—they're stuck in that old traditional mindset—and they think that they're making themselves relevant for the future, and they're actually not. They're not leaning into abundance, not leaning into a world where you have access to all the experts that you need to make yourself indispensable.

It's really interesting. You sit around in meetings all day, unhappy and working on tasks you do not enjoy and not giving up control, and I equate it to eating comfort food. In the long run if you eat nothing but comfort food it's not any good, but if you lean into this world where there is abundance...wow.

Imagine if you and your team could do 10x the work that you could do today for the same cost to the company. Everybody's got a backlog. I met this designer the other day and he's like, "Yeah, I've got a long backlog, but no I can't use the Gig Economy." It doesn't make any sense! He's drowning in the ocean and refuses to board the lifeboat!

Look at the person that's looking to disrupt, not protect. In organizations where we have the most success, if you find that person that wants to disrupt, that's not looking to protect himself, follow him. He's looking to blow things up and change them, to make an impact, and usually that's a go-getter within an organization that's trying to drive change.

If you join that person, join that disruption, your career can take off. I used to always say to people, "You should measure your success on the amount of promotions your customers get." Consider yourself a successful thought leader by how you drive disruption. It's also about staying relevant. If you don't change and the world changes around you, it may be too late.

The last thing is about support. Why do so many people struggle when changing their mindsets or lifestyle? Some of it is dedication, but a lot is based around emotion and distraction.

Paul: The Busy Trap.

Mike: Exactly. That's why you need support. You need to share your mindset and your goals with the people around you, the people you trust. When you start to doubt yourself, or you get distracted, or you get worn down, they are the ones who will pick you back up. That's how you stay motivated and stay on track for success. If you set your mind to practice the T.I.D.E. model every day, taskifying and delegating and evolving, you'd be a leader in no time. You couldn't be stopped.

So why don't you?

STEVE RADER

Paul: What is the biggest myth you've heard about the Gig Economy?

Steve: I think the number one myth that most people believe is that the freelance market consists of unskilled teenagers in their basement who have nothing to offer you and can't possibly understand your problems. Plus, if they have all this time on their hands, why don't they get a real job? Those assumptions are just wrong.

A lot of these freelancers do have full-time jobs. I think

what's surprising to some companies is that their workforce is actually on these platforms, too.

There's a great story. Topcoder was purchased by WiPro, this big multinational corporation. They provide information technology, consulting, and business process services. It's about $8 billion in revenue, so we're talking a huge company. And they use what is essentially the Gig Mindset as a part of their strategy.

Mike Morris will tell you they basically looked at their user base at Topcoder and realized that several hundred of the WiPro employees were actually on Topcoder, and had been doing work with their WiPro emails. Their work emails. They were actually working Topcoder challenges while at work using work resources.

WiPro said, "You know what? That's great. Because we don't look at it as they're doing work for other people, we look at it as they're learning. They're learning how to do things better."

People forget that the average productivity of a company employee is three out of every eight hours. What are those people doing with the other five hours? Well, some of them are actually being productive and learning. WiPro gave all those people bonuses and recognized them in the company.

I think that's a great model for companies. They ought to be thinking in terms of how they give their employees opportunities to grow and become more innovative and to really be assets that are happy and contributing. So what if somebody else is paying them? Think about it. You're not paying for that training. It's kind of a win-win.

Going back to those myths, I think they have been blown out of proportion. They usually come from people who have not tried this new way of working, or thought it was an easy fix. I just don't believe myths anymore. I think about a Topcoder or a Tongal where the people that join those communities have already taken a step to say, "I'm interested in this enough to create an account." That's actually a pretty big bar, at least for me.

That already puts them well ahead of the curve for anybody else in that domain. It means they have something, a fire in their gut to go *do* something.

Clay Shirky's book, *Cognitive Surplus*, was an interesting one for me. He pointed out that when we went to the eight-hour work week, people suddenly had lots of free time. It used to be that your job was 90 percent of your life. You woke up, you worked, you came home, you ate, you went to bed. Suddenly, we limit work to eight hours. Now that worker has time to be with their family, time to learn a new skill, time to start their own business. What's interesting is what happens culturally.

If you tell your buddy, "Hey, yeah, I went to an NFL game this weekend and I spent seven hours and $150," they go, "Oh, that's great." If you say, "Hey, I went to a Topcoder hackathon and I actually did this coding thing where I coded for five or six hours straight, or maybe even longer," people look at you like *Why would you do that?* That's like doing work on your time off.

But when it's your passion, that's what you want to be doing. People don't blink an eye if you go waste your time, but they seem to have this cultural issue with doing activities that you enjoy and fill you up.

The point is that people are using their time to make more money, or gain new skills. They can practice and get better and make themselves relevant. That's what the Gig Economy allows.

DYAN FINKHOUSEN

Paul: We talked a lot about myths in this chapter, but what about the tools and tips people need to succeed?

Dyan: The Gig Economy is a large, complex, rapidly evolving space. If you don't have a good listening system in place, you can quickly fall behind pace. Maintaining research on the Gig Economy and augmenting your own experience base by collaborating with your network on best practices will help you succeed with the toolkit. We were able to amplify our learning, refine our operational excellence and accelerate our scaling process by creating a centralized team responsible for Gig Economy engagement and operations.

Many organizations are concerned about the administrative burden and the compliance risk associated with leveraging the gig marketplace. Companies are concerned that using gig resources to scale causes an administrative problem. Suddenly your workforce is enormous. How are you supposed to manage that, to keep track of all those resources?

My group has designed gig operations to make it easy for these teams to access freelancers, experts. We manage gig marketplace vendor contracts, onboarding, operations, and payments.

By building and managing the operational framework for gig resource engagement—the expert operating system— we enable our business teams to focus simply on their business missions, in collaboration with the experts we help them recruit.

So that's a consistent theme for best practices as our

teams learn the art of giving up control. We make it easier for our business teams by establishing master services agreements, purchase orders, vendor and freelancer payments, expert collaboration processes, and running interference for any questions or concerns that might arise.

We help recruit the right experts because we are able to translate between the two worlds: the marketplace world and the heavy industrial world. That is super helpful. The sponsor teams can focus on the mission and focus on giving feedback to the expert resource and integrating the work that the expert resource does.

So in terms of best practices, again, to evolve and scale the use of gig resources, that administrative layer has been incredibly helpful for just about every team that we've worked with. We've created a hyperlink from mission to expert.

Another quick example—in this case, a marketing team that came to us and said, "Hey, we're resource constrained, running with our hair on fire. We need help in a lot of different areas, but we can't spend six months writing up a contract for every project that we need help with."

Sound familiar?

So we set this team up with access to the Upwork platform. We got the accounting squared away so that we knew what accounting codes to use for which types of projects. And this team used our platform for the vast majority of their marketing and communications support needs.

The team ran about 110 tests through this blueprint model in 2018. They went through all four steps of T.I.D.E. Those tests ranged from the creation of videos, the creation of templates, whether they're word templates or slide show templates. There was a lot of translation work, ad development, copywriting, proofreading, creation of social reel, just a lot of high-velocity, high-quality, low-touch types of work to support this team's needs throughout the course of the year.

So very specifically, the team would identify a task; they would post the parameters of what they needed help with on the platform.

They would take a look through the experts that responded to their posts and interview and hire the experts on the platform, and basically get the work done quickly. My team would pay Upwork on a monthly basis and then just settle up those charges with this marketing team. So the team was empowered to engage experts for the tasks that they needed help with, and we would just settle up behind the scenes on a monthly basis to make sure Upwork was getting paid for the work.

It was an incredibly streamlined, agile process for the team.

Another example—we had a group that needed a whitepaper proofread overnight for an executive event the next day. We had the system preconfigured, with a lot of experts prevetted, so we were able to engage an expert within a couple of hours. The whitepaper was proofread overnight and the executives received a fully polished whitepaper the next day. Just an example of great work, with great agility.

You have a benefit, as the reader holding this book right now. You have an advantage because you're coming in at this moment. At this time. The foundations are already laid out. The infrastructure is already there. You don't have to reinvent the wheel.

Even better, Paul has done the homework. He's already worked to develop his model and tested it on all of us. We learned the basics, we rode with training wheels. Now you can stand on our shoulders and go even higher.

TUCKER MAX

Paul: You talked about myths in the last chapter, Tucker. What would you say to people trying to get started? What are your best practices?

Tucker: First, understand that what works for us won't directly translate for everyone. We engage with freelancers at scale. Most people don't. They are different, and you should not consider them the same, right?

I don't know how many people still have this, but the idea that freelance talent is not quality. That people are freelance because they can't get a full-time job. It's nonsense. We've hired more than 50 percent of our full-time people out of our freelance pool. In fact, we find overall the freelance pool to be far higher talent than the people applying.

We get thousands of people applying to our jobs. I mean, *Entrepreneur* magazine named us the number one company culture in America for a reason. We get thousands of people applying to every job, and we still mostly hire out of our freelance pool. So the talent level is a big myth.

Another one that comes to mind isn't a conscious myth. It is an unconscious myth. There's an idea that a lot of people have that freelancers just know what to do. That's wrong. This is very much about setting expectations.

What happens is people engage with freelancers, and then get shitty results. So they blame the freelancer. They blame freelancers in general, and then you get this myth.

You can hire the best book cover designer on Earth, but if you don't communicate your vision to them, then they can't do a great book cover. You have got to work just as hard as they do at your part of the role, which is communicating what you need them to do, and when, and how. Most people do not. They just don't understand that.

There's another myth that freelancers have a mercenary mindset. Look, you can find freelancers like that, but again in our experience, freelancers are not like that at all. They're normal people. They have the same wants, desires, dreams, goals. In fact, our mission and our culture is what attracts so many high-level freelancers to us and why so many of them will work for us or work with us for less than they will anyone else. Because of the way we treat them and what we stand for, because that's a value. That's a real value to them, and they're willing to pay for that by taking less money than they could potentially get.

The places that are paying them more, it's awful work. They hate it. It's not like we're just paying them less because we're nice. There's more to it. What we do is treat them well, provide services, cater to them the way you would want to be catered to in that situation. If your boss just ragged on you all day, eventually the money isn't worth it. We take care of our freelancers because they are business drivers.

Another myth is a lot of freelancers can have a scarcity mindset. That one is a little true. They can have that sort of, "Oh God. I've got to get my next gig to eat." Now, you can deal with that by working with them individually, as an individual person. Like what we do as a company. You can deal with that, and people can come out of that. Often we have to help our freelancers either deprogram when working with us or when they come on full time, you kind of have to heal them of that.

That's something you should be aware of in dealing with even the best freelancers. If they're struggling to make ends meet or get gigs—or even if they're not—sometimes they'll be in that mindset. It doesn't mean they'll screw you, and it doesn't mean they're bad people. It's just you have to understand you're not their only client. You're not the only thing that's happening in their life. You're not their entire world, so you need to understand that and accommodate that.

Don't get caught up in the myths of the Gig Economy. I love this advice from Simon Sinek: "Dream big. Start small. But most of all, start." The best way to fight the myths is to get out there and try yourself.

It's time for you to level up your life, to reclaim the time that's rightfully yours. Look back at where you were when you first picked up this book. I'll bet you were frustrated. I know I was, all those years ago. I knew that there was a better way to work. A better way to live. I hope that I've shown you just that.

Where you go from here is up to you. I can promise you that it will require your time and your work in order to get it started. The tools are all available. The freelancers are waiting. Just internalize that message from the plaque on President Obama's desk: Hard work is hard. And remember that hard work produces great results.

Let's reimagine what's possible.

CONCLUSION

"'Someday' is a disease that will take your dreams to the grave with you."

—TIM FERRISS, *THE 4-HOUR WORKWEEK: ESCAPE 9-5, LIVE ANYWHERE, AND JOIN THE NEW RICH*

Years ago, I sat down at a coffee shop across from my boss and saw my career flash before my eyes. I was in trouble. The world had changed beneath my feet, and I felt unskilled and unprepared to stay relevant. I wanted to make an impact, to have purpose and meaning, but I also wanted to be a part of my family's journey. I realized that something had to change if any of that was going to be possible. I had to change myself.

Since then, I've given up so many fears and concerns that I once had. I'm not held back by countless meetings or overwhelmed by busywork. My Should List never grows out of control, and my passion projects are pursued and explored. The best part? I get to spend my time on the people who matter most: my family and friends.

The Gig Mindset came out of necessity. I saw the world changing and opted to change with it. My father and grandfather had a path that worked for them, but I had to make my own. I had to adapt. To evolve.

I reset my defaults, shaking loose every myth and fear that I'd had about working with the Gig Economy. What I discovered changed everything. I found a new team waiting online, all around the world, and they were eager and able to help me at every turn. They were my virtual assistants, my researchers, my experts on several subjects. They enabled me because I put my trust in them.

With this newfound freedom and time, I was able to reskill. I taught myself a new model for engaging with this economy, the T.I.D.E. Model. I broke down my projects, identified my experts, and practiced delegation. As I grew more confident, my methods and mindset evolved. I leaned into the turn and accelerated. Instead of just using this mindset for myself, I shared it with my company. I shared it with everyone I met. And to my absolute delight, it caught on.

You've heard from thought leaders from GE and Topcoder and Scribe and NASA. You've experimented yourself with the tasks I provided. You've seen just what this mind-set can do firsthand. Now it's time for you to take the next step.

A NEW WORLD AWAITS

Armed with the knowledge from this book, you have to commit to the new mindset. Every single day wake up and try something new. I've provided one hundred tasks that you can use to start your journey. All you must do is try.

Tomorrow morning, I hope you're going to wake up and feel refreshed. You're going to pick a task and reach out into the gig marketplace to find your expert and start to build your trusted network of freelancers. You're going to do amazing things, and you'll see just what is possible when you reset your defaults.

Tomorrow, you're going to have a virtual assistant book your travel, or engage with an expert to research a difficult topic, or build a team to organize your website, or find the right person to train you on starting a podcast. You'll start to build a network to research competitive strategies, design presentations, or pull content that fits your company's brand. It doesn't matter what your passion project is, the right people are out there waiting to meet you.

Once you have a few projects under your belt, I want you

to contact me via LinkedIn. Let me know what you've been able to do since you started living the Gig Mindset. Share your success stories with others and see just how inspired they'll be. You're not just a student now; you're an ambassador.

Change starts with action. A lot of us feel stuck, feel like we're caught in the Busy Trap. We have no time for ourselves, no time to reskill and pursue the goals we really want. What I'm doing now would have seemed impossible to me just a few years ago. What you'll do tomorrow will change your life.

INSATIABLE CURIOSITY

I had a good friend and mentor—Matt Bencke—pass away not long ago of pancreatic cancer. He was the CEO of an AI startup called Mighty AI here in Seattle. Just an incredible guy, a force of nature. I think I truly realized just how influential he was for me.

I remember walking with him some time ago, and I was complaining about some politics that was going on in the office. I was frustrated about some meeting—or something equally ridiculous. The everyday annoyances all piled up, and I was ready to be done with it.

There was no time for me, for personal growth. I felt like

I was so far behind there was no way to catch up, and the thought of that knowledge gap infuriated me.

Matt laughed. He asked me when I'd lost my perspective. Then he taught me something that sticks with me to this day.

He showed me the power of insatiable curiosity. Always be curious. Continue to learn and continue to grow. He told me that would help me stay relevant. That would help me feel safe. And that would help me find purpose.

Matt was passionate about the idea of a world full of experts being able to accelerate technological advances and make the world better. He taught me that time is precious and fleeting. He made me think about how I spent moments—not days, weeks and years. And he taught me to fight: for time with my family, for time with my friends, to have a career that had purpose.

Somewhere between joining the corporate world and getting tangled in the Busy Trap, I'd forgotten that learning was fun. That being curious is freeing. That being curious allows you to be empathetic and to listen and to truly embrace diversity of thought.

That curiosity allows me to respect everyone's ideas and what everyone can bring to the table, because the chances are that it will make the idea better. That it'll make the work better. That'll I learn something.

Matt inspires the work I do every day. The most important lesson I learned from him, what I'll always carry with me, was insatiable curiosity.

It's the most powerful piece of career advice I've ever received. So if I can leave you with anything, if you walk away from this book with only one bit of new knowledge, it has to be this: continuing to learn and grow is what has given me safety and made me believe that I'm going to stay relevant.

The Gig Economy is as big as the internet, as big as the mobile revolution, as big as a PC on every desk. Every person in every company needs to have a Gig Economy strategy. Matt was very passionate that a world full of experts could accelerate technological advances and make the world better. He dedicated his time as CEO of Mighty AI to that cause.

I think everyone has known loss in their life. They maybe know someone who passed that's impactful to them. So I keep a gift by my desk that Matt gave me to remind me every day that tomorrow is not a given.

That's why it is so important to reclaim your time. It is

so important to have the space you need to do what's important. There are no guarantees about what tomorrow may bring. Take every moment and make it worthwhile.

GIVING PEOPLE WORK

I'll leave you with one last thought.

I'm not keeping all the profits from this book. I am very fortunate that my job and my passion keep my family comfortable. My work pays the bills and puts food on the table. This book was never about making money. I truly believe that everyone needs to learn about the Gig Economy and the Gig Mindset.

That's why a portion of the profit goes to Samasource.

A while back, I read a book by an entrepreneur named Leila Janah called *Give Work*. I was reading while rocking my daughter, and I started to hope she would be able to make a dent in the universe. Leila inspires me with her relentlessness passion. She could have gone to Facebook or another Big Tech company and made millions. Instead, she set out to change the world and bring opportunity to those who need it most.

Her work is really focused on some of the poorest people on the planet. The question of the book is this: how do we solve poverty? She says, "Giving people work—not giving them money—giving them work is one of the most powerful things that we can do. It gives people purpose. It gives them skills. It gives them a way to sustain a lifestyle. It brings them out of poverty and can change the community."

It made me think about my own journey here in the United States. I'm originally from New Orleans, and I had to leave my family to find opportunity. It is hard, and my girls do not get to see their grandparents as often as we'd like. I am fortunate, I don't doubt that, but with modern technology I should have more flexibility. Large companies are trying their best to accommodate employees, but it's still a major challenge.

One of the biggest challenges we face as a nation and in the world is the distribution of opportunity. We have to make sure that opportunity is not only found in tech hubs like San Francisco or Seattle or New York or Boston. Or only in the United States, for that matter. Opportunity should be worldwide.

The goal is that everyone who has skills, everyone who has something to give, is given the opportunity to participate in making the world a better place. And that open participation, that diversity of thought, that diversity of background, that diversity of experience is critical to making sure that we make products and projects that are inclusive.

When we listen to each other, when we welcome in a diverse array of our community, we build a better world. We create opportunity for those who might have otherwise gone unnoticed. We shine a light on the talent and creativity that exists all around us. It's a benefit that this diversity of thought leads to better products, but the journey is just as important. We're empowering the talent of tomorrow and giving them a platform to excel. That's powerful.

That's what the Gig Mindset can do. That's what you can do.

My father and grandfather followed the corporate path, and it provided for our family. They walked a line that is radically changing and slowly disappearing. The new way forward requires more flexibility and a different perspective. It requires you to embrace the Gig Economy and engage with freelancers around the world. I did it, and so can you.

Reclaim your time. Reinvent your career. And ride the next wave of disruption.

When you first picked up this book, you stood in quicksand. The Gig Mindset just threw you a rope. Are you ready to grab ahold?

APPENDIX A—FIFTY TASKS FOR WORK

I know that this can all seem overwhelming, and sometimes we just don't know how to begin.

Here are fifty projects I've completed on Fiverr over the last few years. Use these ideas as inspiration to see the potential of the Gig Economy and what it means to be an air traffic controller.

BUSINESS

1. I'm looking for a spreadsheet that helps calculate savings based on extra principal payments. I currently have a thirty-year fixed mortgage and want to know how I can pay it off in fifteen years.

2. Suggest five memorable, SEO-friendly domain names.

3. I need market research done for sixteen items. Some of the information can be added from Crunchbase.

4. I'm looking to understand texting behavior for US consumers compared to email or phone communication. Please provide trends and a demographic breakdown of people who text.

5. I would like a script that supports the technology disruptions that provide value to consumers and businesses.

6. I'm looking to create an infographic that shows two emerging ecosystems of companies. Please identify the trends, market size, and leaders of SaaS companies working on solving scheduling and SMS-based companies working to reach customers via text.

7. Can you please update these slides with new information?

8. Can you create an Excel spreadsheet of all products available on this website including brand, price, and product description?

9. I'm looking for two classifications of sites: e-learning sites that offer classes and sites where people can get help via video or chat.

10. I'm planning a trip with six college friends to Breck-enridge, Colorado July 9–13. Please find ten available Airbnbs with at least five bedrooms. Compile a list of properties with links, total cost per person, and a few sentences about the amenities.

11. I'm looking for a summary of Microsoft Office prod-ucts communities. This should include LinkedIn groups and YouTube channels. Please provide the name of the group/channel, the number of subscrib-ers, and links in an Excel spreadsheet.

12. I am looking for a list of news articles about the future of remote work.

13. I need to transfer the data table in slides eight and nine of the attached PDF to Excel.

14. I need someone to create a new slide with all of the listed companies' logos. You'll have to search the web to find each one.

15. I'm adding a list of the books I've read to my website. I need someone to write a short blurb (no more than thirty characters) for each of the thirty-nine books. You can use book summaries on Amazon.

16. I have a two-step project that should take two hours in

total. Step one: See if the companies on the attached list are on the spreadsheet. If they are, add either B2B or B2C in column D. If they are not, add the company name into Column B and the B2B/B2C designation into Column D. Step two. Fill in the additional columns.

17. Can you research sources for statistics listed in a slideshow presentation?

DIGITAL/ONLINE MARKETING

18. I am looking for ten recommendations on available names on Twitter.

19. I need someone to recommend articles for my Twitter feed to support posting two times per day.

GRAPHICS AND DESIGN

20. I'm looking to create a book cover to put on my website to advertise that it's coming soon. The book is called *Gig Mindset* with a tagline of *Reclaim Time, Rethink What's Possible*. I've attached an image I think would be good for the cover.

21. I need an avatar cartoon created in *South Park* style.

22. I need a movie poster for a screenplay I'm working on

called *Searching for Ocho* with the tagline "The incrementalist revolution." It's about a big corporation's search to create an eight-blade razor.

23. I need five logo concepts for Telamentor.

24. I am looking for a logo for my new blog header. I've attached some examples of fonts and designs I like.

25. I'm launching a podcast and need someone to find an image for each episode. I need eight engaging images with the same tone.

26. I need to find headshots for each thought leader on the attached list and format them to 300px x 300px.

27. I'm new to YouTube and want to create a channel that curates videos from my niche. I will have a few original videos.

28. I'm looking to create a version of the attached shirt that says "Start Something." The words can be stacked with a company logo, similar to the attached.

PROGRAMMING AND TECH

29. Please research the best options for building a custom PC per the designated requirements.

30. Can you create something similar to this web-site, but in your style? I want something elegant and simple with a place to collect people's email addresses.

31. I'm looking for an editable email template I can use in Microsoft Outlook. I would like the delivery to be an .msg file I can populate and send.

32. I purchased a theme and a plug-in for my new website and need help loading the new theme, adding a logo, and customizing the layout.

33. Can you back up website files to Dropbox?

34. I need a WordPress developer to update my current site by changing the tagline, adding a multistep form, and putting category headings at the top of the page.

WRITING AND TRANSLATION

35. I need an article written about the blog I'm getting ready to launch.

36. Using the attached articles for reference, write an article about the rise of the Gig Economy and how it's not a fad. Please include links to articles you reference.

37. I need content written for the About page on my new website.

38. I'm launching a site and need a copywriter to produce six taglines and supporting blurbs for the various pages. Attached is a current sample of the site.

39. I need an explainer video script for a new idea.

40. I need to get some research on the best practices when hiring freelancers.

41. I am looking to write an e-book that teaches people how to work with freelancers. This includes the benefits, challenges, and tips and tricks. I've attached a draft of my current thinking, as well as some supporting resources. I'm looking for a solid outline with supporting points for each chapter.

42. I need a bio to be submitted to the Social Venture Partners website.

43. Please proofread this document.

44. I need someone to research mentoring for business coaching sites and directories.

45. I need my resumé updated.

46. Can you transcribe this file and put it into a Word document?

47. I need a document translated from Chinese to English.

48. I am doing a social post that talks about how much time people waste at work and have attached some data points. Can you provide an infographic that can be used along with the post?

49. I am publishing a book and need to create a landing page that can capture people's email addresses and provide links to purchase on Amazon when it is available. I have attached the assets and some sample sites that I like.

50. I publish a weekly newsletter and need assistance in writing a few-sentence summary of each article. There will be eight articles in each edition.

APPENDIX B—FIFTY TASKS FOR HOME

SCHEDULE APPOINTMENTS

1. Can you please call Dr. Xyz and find the earliest appointment? I'm a new patient, but my wife and daughters go to see him. I would prefer an early morning appointment. Once you find three or four available times, I'll ask you to schedule an appointment.

2. Can you please contact Alpine Sprinkler and ask who they recommend for backflow testing? Then contact who they recommend and set up an appointment to do the testing at my house.

3. I'm going to see Dave Matthews on Labor Day weekend at the Gorge Amphitheater. I need to find the

cheapest tickets in section 101 and lower 203 for September 1. I need two tickets next to each other. Can you please provide at least ten options for tickets from a few sites?

4. Please send calendar invites to me and friends for the tennis events below.

5. Can you please contact the Bellevue Water District and report a water leak coming from the meter (image attached)? I would like someone to come out and investigate the issue.

6. The water heater I purchased from Ally Plumbing in 2016 has a broken pilot light. Can you please contact them and schedule someone to come out and fix it? I currently don't have hot water in most of my house and would like to get it addressed today or tomorrow.

7. Please contact the restaurant and cancel my Mother's Day reservation. The number is located on the website below. We have chosen a different option.

8. I'm looking to take my family to iFLY on February 12. There are two families, and we would like to go together. We would like to go in the mid-morning but are flexible on times. I need you to get the info and then book and pay for the tickets.

9. I need to get a reservation for four people at Ishoni (link below) at 6 p.m. on February 10. Call when they open at 5 p.m. to book the reservation.

10. I need tubing reservations for the 9 a.m. session at the Snoqualmie Summit on February 5. We will have four adults, one child, and three kids under five.

HOUSE PROJECTS

11. I need to create a spreadsheet with all the information for a shade quote I received. I filled out the first column as an example. The quote info can be accessed on the link below. Once this is done, I want to get three additional quotes from companies in town.

12. I need quotes from three electricians on installing two electrical outlets—one inside and one outside. Both are on the same wall as existing outlets and light switches.

13. I have a 3,000 square foot house with a detached garage. I'm looking for three quotes on moss removal. I would like the job to be completed in the next few weeks. Once we find a well-rated option, please book the appointment.

WEB RESEARCH

14. I need to find five statistics with supporting sources that show how busy people have become in the past five years. I was planning to use the info below, but the research is dated, and I'm looking for something more current.

15. I'm looking for three additional articles from popular industry and thought leaders on the time wasted in meetings. Please provide summary quotes and thoughts for each article.

16. I'm looking to create a customer four-step form on a WordPress site and need five highly rated plug-ins that can do this. They must send an email when the form is complete, and the data must be able to be downloaded to Excel (CVS file).

17. I need a full list of Gig Economy startups and companies in Israel. Here are two examples to get you started. Please provide a link to the company and its address.

18. I'm writing a blog post on the paradox of choice as it applies to the various tools, service, apps, and products that are available in today's workplace. Please find ten good articles that speak to the challenges this is creating.

19. I'm looking for a list of podcasts that cover Microsoft Excel, Power BI, Tableau, data visualization, and business analytics. Would be great to get twenty if possible.

20. I have an Amazon Prime Chase Bank credit card and need the payment address so I can do bill pay through my bank.

21. I'm looking for ten articles that highlight specific areas where computers/AI are getting better than humans.

22. I'm looking for a list of podcasts that are produced by Microsoft, Google, Adobe, or Salesforce. Please send the information in an Excel spreadsheet containing the name of the podcast and a link to the podcast site.

23. I'm looking for ten case studies showing how a specific company is helping enterprise customers increase productivity and drive their digital transformation. Here are some examples.

24. I'm looking for apps, tools, and websites that help people break projects into tasks. Ideally info/tools that can help people know what to delegate.

25. I need a list of all the podcasts you can find that cover

the Gig Economy, future of work, freelancing, and sharing economy.

26. I'm looking for companies and thought leaders that have a page on recommended books on their given subject area. I'm specifically interested in understanding the various web layouts and designs for these pages. Can you please find twenty sites?

27. I'm launching a podcast of interviews with industry leaders. I want to find some articles that outline best practices for developing compelling questions.

28. I want to cancel my Delta Airlines American Express card. I need to know when they issue the companion ticket and when they charge the annual fee.

29. I need research for an article I'm writing about exploring ways people can calculate how much their time is worth. Can you please find five to ten articles on this topic and provide ten bullet summaries?

30. I just got a Lenovo ThinkCentre M910q and want to plug in all three of my monitors. They don't have HDMI ports, just DVI. What is the best option for getting this done?

PURCHASE AND SELL ITEMS

31. I'm looking to sell an iWatch series 2 38MM with a white band. Can you write an advertisement, get a recommended price, and post it to Craigslist and eBay? It's preowned but has rarely been used.

32. I need to purchase a clip for the right side of my dishwasher. Can you please call Pacific Specialty and have the part delivered to my house? Here are the model and serial numbers for my washer.

33. I have a couch (image below), and two of the buttons came off. Can you please search and get three quotes on what it would take to fix the couch? I've attached images.

34. I need toilet flapper replacements for two Kohler toilets. Please use the attached serial numbers to find a flapper part with the lowest price, purchase the item, and ship it to my house.

35. I am looking for the best place to purchase bulk LEGO sets. These should include miniature characters, and the pieces should be washed and various colors and a variety of parts. Please provide ten links to sets that are between two and five pounds. Make sure the pricing includes shipping to my house.

36. Can you look at the two links below and create an Excel file that combines the reading list on both sites? Please include the name of the book and the Amazon link.

37. I'm working on a blog article and need to create a file with all the company's images for a week of listings on Product Hunt. I'm trying to show how many new products launch weekly. Please deliver the package in a zip file.

PRODUCT RESEARCH

38. The handle on my Victorinox bag broke on a trip this week. The screws got loose and the rod came out of the handle housing. I need to find the best way to get it repaired either from the company or a place in Bellevue.

39. I'm looking to get a mesh Wi-Fi network in my house. Please send me some reviews of the eero and Google Wi-Fi systems and the best price on each.

40. I'm looking for an umbrella base that will go under a table, like the one below. I'm trying to find something smaller than seventeen inches square.

41. I just moved into an open office and am looking for

a pair of wireless over-ear headphones that have a charging dock. Can you provide ten options and have at least five of them be vintage? Each one in the list should have four-plus star reviews.

42. I purchased an iPhone through AT&T about six months ago and am having issues with the GPS. I've tried all of the recommended software fixes. Can you contact AT&T and let me know my options on getting a new phone?

43. I'm looking for white cantilever umbrellas like the one below. Can you provide a list of at least ten options?

44. I'm looking for reviews that compare shirts from MTailor and Untuckit. Please provide your point of view on which one is best based on your research.

45. I need a price comparison and rating comparison for all the attached modems.

46. I'm looking for a podcast kit (two mics with stands and screens, mixer, and headphones). I would like to get five to ten options that have great ratings.

47. I'm looking for this American Giant T-shirt that is out of stock. Can you see if you can find it or contact American Giant to see when they will have it in stock?

BOOK TRAVEL

48. I'm looking for flights from Seattle to NYC on June 24 and returning July 7. I prefer nonstop and would like to fly Delta or Alaska if possible.

49. I'm looking for the cheapest flights based on this information...Please provide five quotes that include all appropriate fees and taxes.

50. I need two plane tickets from Seattle to Washington, DC, on April 1. Nonstop flight preferred, can be either red-eye or first thing in the morning on Delta if possible. Must arrive by 3 p.m. local time. Send me three to five options.

ABOUT THE AUTHOR

A few years ago, **PAUL ESTES** was juggling a high-stress job and a young family. Both he and his wife worked full time. Something had to give. A friend recommended he hire a virtual assistant. That decision changed his life, reinventing the way he worked, lived, and thought.

Today, Paul is an unstoppable advocate for the Gig Economy. He's relentlessly curious, ridiculously energetic, and radically passionate about inspiring others to embrace *their* profound potential in the 'future of work'. By accessing a global pool of talent, Paul believes every person can find time to reskill, reinvent, and be exponential.

His mantra is "Reclaim your time. Rethink what is possible."

After twenty years in Big Tech—driving deals and transformation at Dell, Amazon, and Microsoft—Paul transitioned into working as an independent remote freelancer focused on helping companies implement Gig Economy programs, freelance programs, and remote work strategies. He also shares his insights from main-stages as a keynote speaker and panelist at conferences, and he provides thoughts and advice via LinkedIn articles.

Outside of work, Paul is passionate about enjoying quality time with his wife and two amazing daughters. He practices what he teaches by engaging with experts in the freelance space who help him better allocate his time at work and at home.

ACKNOWLEDGMENTS

This book is dedicated to my amazing wife, Rachel, and my daughters, Sydney and Harper. May they lead fulfilling, healthy, and purposeful lives when they enter the world of work.

While this book has been a labor of the past two years, the effort leading up to it lasted much longer. I realized long ago that there had to be a better way to work, a better way to move forward alongside technology and the changing economy. On my journey, I met many amazing people who shared that feeling. Without them and their unwavering support, I don't believe this book would have come to be.

- To the hundreds of amazing freelancers who help me with personal projects over the past five years. Your passion, dedication, work ethic, and curiosity forever changed how I view the future.

- My wife, Rachel, for being my rock, biggest fan, and biggest critic. Always pushing me to rethink where we are headed.

- My parents, John and Peggy Estes, for providing an amazing upbringing, unconditional love, support, and drive for curiosity by supporting all the ever-changing interests I had growing up.

- My sister, Sara, her husband, Justin, and amazing daughters, Emma and Julia, who I miss often and work so that they can all have the opportunities that I have in Seattle without having to leave.

- My amazing in-laws, Roy and Susan Bachmann, Jared and Alisa Klustner, and their son, Micky.

- My two career coaches, Samia Kornweibel and Donna Sellers, who taught me that asking for career help is a necessary if you want to chart a new path.

- Ted Roden, Joshua Boltuch, and all of the amazing virtual assistants at Fancy Hands who have saved me over eleven days in the past eighteen months by helping with tons of tasks.

- Kathy Gatley, whose storytelling gift has helped me

find my voice and pushed me to be vulnerable when sharing my personal journey.

- Matt Bencke, whose life inspires my work every day, helps me appreciate the little things, and the courage to reinvent my own path by seeing where curiosity takes me.

- Adam Benzion, whose recommendation to hire a virtual assistant put me on the path to the Gig Mindset and whose journey from corporate America to serial entrepreneurship inspires my work daily.

- Leslie Friend, who has always been on the other end of the line to hear all my crazy ideas and support the good times and bad. Her passion for seeing the world while working remotely has pushed me to think that there are different ways to find balance between life and work.

- Many mentors who have shared their experiences and shaped my professional journey. John Medica, Mark Vena, Michelle Pearcy, Nino Storniolo, Bryan Tobey, and Chris Nelson.

- Allyn Schinski who entered our life five years ago and has become a part of the family, providing words of wisdom every day.

- Kelly Tregillus (strategic account director at Upwork), who responded to my cold call to the company 1-800 number and had the patience to wade through my excitement about the potential of engaging with freelancers.

- The team at Upwork who is fighting every day to help large companies unlock the power of engaging with freelancers to create Work Without Limits™: Stephane Kasriel, Eric Gilpin, Hayden Brown, Don Forest, Bonnie (Elgamil) Sherman, Maida (Marar) Kasper, John Oliver, and many more.

- John Younger, whose writing and work have helped me understand the potential of a blended workforce.

- All the contributors to the book who have shared their stories and truly believe in the power of the Gig Mindset: Mike Morris, Steve Rader, Dyan Finkhousen, John Winsor, and Tucker Max.